SPEED LEARNING CARTOMANCY
FORTUNE TELLING WITH PLAYING CARDS

GRAB THE AUDIOBOOK FROM
HTTP://THECOLDREADINGCOMPANY.CO.UK
COMPLETELY FREE!

THIS MANUSCRIPT
COPYRIGHT 2011 JULIAN MOORE

FIRST EDITION APRIL 2011 REVISION ONE

JULIAN@THECOLDREADINGCOMPANY.CO.UK
WWW.THECOLDREADINGCOMPANY.CO.UK

TABLE OF CONTENTS

BEFORE WE START	4
OVERVIEW	5
CHAPTER 1 - THE FOUR SUITS	6
DIAMONDS AND HEARTS	6
CLUBS AND SPADES	8
REVISION: CHAPTER ONE	13
CHAPTER 2 - PUTTING THE SUITS TOGETHER	14
REVISION: CHAPTER TWO	18
CHAPTER 3 - THREE CARD SUIT READINGS	19
COLOUR READINGS	19
QUESTIONS : CHAPTER THREE	22
CHAPTER 4 - THE SPOT CARDS	23
REVISION: CHAPTER FOUR	30
CHAPTER 5 - DECIPHERING THE SPOT CARDS	31
REVISION: CHAPTER FIVE	35
REVISION STOP: CHAPTERS ONE TO FIVE	36
CHAPTER 6 - THREE CARD READINGS	37
CHAPTER 7 - THE COURT CARDS	52
THE COURT DIAMONDS	53
THE COURT CLUBS	53
THE COURT HEARTS	54
THE COURT SPADES	54
CHAPTER 8 - DECK PERSONALITY	68
WHICH COURT CARD ARE YOU?	68
WHICH SPOT CARDS ARE YOU?	69

    WHICH SPOT CARDS DESCRIBE YOUR CURRENT SITUATION? 70

    WHICH SPOT CARDS DESCRIBE YOUR 'PERFECT OUTCOME'? 72

CHAPTER 9 - MORE ON READINGS — 75

    CHOOSING THE CARDS — 75

    GENERAL READINGS VS QUESTION READINGS — 75

    GETTING UNSTUCK — 76

    CREATING CONVERSATION — 76

CHAPTER 10 - BEYOND THE 3 CARD READING — 78

    THE NINE CARD READING — 78

    THE SEVENS SPREAD — 79

    THE STAR SPREAD — 80

    OTHER SPREADS — 80

CHAPTER 11 - NUMEROLOGY AND OTHER SYSTEMS — 81

CHAPTER 12 - CARTOMANCY AS LANGUAGE — 84

CHAPTER 13 - CONCLUSION — 86

BEFORE WE START

This book is very hands-on and as such you're going to need two packs of playing cards, one of which you're going to be defacing with a permanent marker pen. This will become your personal 'working pack' which you will be using to remember the meanings of the cards as you go. I recommend using a thin-tipped marker pen as you will probably end up with quite a few scribbles on each card by the time we're done.

We will be adding words and descriptions to this working pack throughout the learning process and it can be used while you're learning as a memory aid for when you're giving your first readings, and as time goes on can be enhanced with your own personal thoughts and insights about the cards as you work with them.

If you go for a while without giving a cartomancy reading or need a quick refresher at some time in the future, your working pack will always be there for you to jog your memory and provide an easy way to get back up to speed with your readings.

You will be switching between your working pack and the normal pack as you learn to read the cards so that you do not become too dependant on your working pack. However you will find that your working pack may well take on a life of it's own and you may become very attached to it!

There's something nice about having a pack of cards that you've personalised with your own scribbles and ideas, and I see no problem with using your working pack in readings - it can actually help engage the person you are giving a reading to because, unlike many of the illustrated Tarot packs whose pictures and symbols people can relate to, playing cards can seem rather abstract. Having your own meanings and concepts written on the faces of the cards can help other people get more involved in their own readings.

So grab a couple of packs of cards and a marker pen and let's get started!

CALL TO ACTION!

THROUGHOUT THIS BOOK YOU WILL SEE THE WORD

ACTION

THIS MEANS YOU HAVE TO ACTUALLY DO SOMETHING

MAKE SURE YOU DO EVERYTHING YOU ARE ASKED TO DO WHEN CALLED UPON TO ACT

YOU WILL LEARN MUCH FASTER THIS WAY

OVERVIEW

Even if you've never given cartomancy much thought in the past, you're probably aware or have heard that during a playing card reading the suits mean one thing, the numbers one to ten mean another and the court cards represent people.

This is the basic idea of playing card readings - the four suits each represent a concept, the numbers one to ten each have their own meaning based on numerology, and the court cards each represent a certain type of man, woman or youth depending on their suit.

However, it is this apparent simplicity that can make learning the meanings of the cards so difficult - lists and descriptions of these meanings can easily be read from pages in a book one evening and forgotten the next. We need to think deeply about each number and engage with each suit. If we understand the connections between the numbers and suits of each card we will find them easier to remember. We need to create some relevance for ourselves - you can't remember stuff that your brain hasn't engaged with.

Many people find learning the numerology meanings of the numbers one to ten impossibly difficult, even though on the face of it it should be a simple task. Yet making the number meanings stick in the mind, even though there's only ten of them, seems to be a major stumbling block for many people learning numerology and therefore cartomancy itself.

What most people don't realise is that the suits alone can become the basis of a simple yet effective reading, and the interaction of the suits are just as important as the numbers. The great thing about this is that there are only four suits so there's hardly anything to learn, and if during a reading you have a memory lapse about what the numbers mean you've always got the suits to fall back on.

Ultimately we need to learn how to 'give a reading'. There are two main types of readings - the all purpose reading and the question reading. All purpose readings are 'one size fits all' readings for people with no specific questions who simply want some insight into their current situation, whereas question readings are far more specific - people hold a current problem or circumstance in their mind while the reading is conducted. Throughout your time getting to know the cards you should experiment with both kinds of readings, sometimes just 'see what the cards say' about things in general and at other times hold a 'question' in mind that you'd like some insight on while you are using the cards.

Of course to give yourself even the most basic reading you're going to need to know a bit about the cards, and the best place to start is with the four suits of Diamonds, Clubs, Hearts and Spades.

CHAPTER 1 - THE FOUR SUITS

There are four suits in a normal pack of playing cards - Diamonds, Clubs, Hearts and Spades. It is widely understood, even by people who have never given a reading with cards, that Diamonds means 'money' and Hearts mean 'love'. Many people have also picked up the idea that the Ace Of Spades means death and that all the Spades mean bad luck. Most people don't have any idea what Clubs mean!

With this 'common knowledge' in mind, we're going to start by keeping things really simple using these meanings for the red suits. Try and imagine each description in your own mind to create a really vivid picture for each one. The idea is that instead of thinking of just one word when you think of a suit you in fact conjure up a variety of concepts.

Diamonds and Hearts

The two 'simplest' suits to grasp are the red suits of Diamonds and Hearts, simply because they both have names that are fairly self-explanatory.

♦ **Diamonds**

- **Money** - Diamonds conjure up images of vast wealth, jewels and treasures
- **Success**: Wealth and success usually go hand in hand
- **Power**: With wealth comes the power of emperors and kings
- **Energy**: Diamonds are almost indestructible and able to cut through anything!

♥ **Hearts**

- **Love** - The heart is the universal symbol of love
- **Emotions**: We may think with our heads, but we follow our hearts
- **Healing**: The power of love to heal all wounds
- **Pleasure**: There's love and there's lust!

```
TOP TIP: IT IS LARGELY RECOGNISED THAT THERE'S NOTHING INHERENTLY 'BAD'
ABOUT RED SUITS AND AN EASY RULE TO FOLLOW IS 'RED IS GOOD'.
```

Action: Take out the Ace of Diamonds and Ace of Hearts from what is to be your 'working pack' and write the four descriptions for each suit on each side alongside the four corners of each card as illustrated.

For now don't worry about what the Aces 'mean' - at the moment we're only interested in the suits of Diamonds and Hearts. Let's imagine you are giving an all purpose card reading for yourself and the first card you turn over is a Heart.

Action: Place the Ace of Hearts face up in front of you.

♥   You are immediately drawn to ideas of love, romance, personal relationships and all the other things you have associated with the suit of Hearts. But so what? We have the idea, the notion of Hearts staring at us, but what about it?

To make sense of this first card we need a second card to show us where this is going and what influences are being brought to bare on this idea. With a second card we can turn a simple concept into a situation.

Action: Place the Ace of Diamonds face up next to the Ace of Hearts.

♥♦   This second card lends some clarification to our original Heart card. There's money involved, or some kind of success tied in with the idea of love. The first card, the Heart is the MAIN FOCUS. But this second card, the Diamond, is shedding some light on exactly WHAT it's all about.

Let's just think for a moment about what this could all mean:

- A partnership you are in could be about to come into some money
- A lover you have yet to meet may well be wealthy
- If you follow the work you love it may reap rewards
- Your family's current endeavours could come to fruition

Those are just examples off the top of my head. I quite literally sat here trying to figure out what it could mean. With only two suits, one in front of the other, I have begun a train of thought as I try and create meaning from what is in front of me.

And this is exactly as it should be. I'm not 'looking up' the cards on a list, I'm not referring to some diagram or some dusty tome on cartomancy. I'm simply giving myself the space to work out what two concepts, Hearts and Diamonds, mean to me given that the first card is 'the subject' and the second card is 'shedding light' on the subject.

But what if the cards were the other way around?

Action: Pick up the Ace of Hearts and the Ace of Diamonds. This time, place the Ace of Diamonds down first.

♦   With the Diamond being the focus we are drawn to ideas of money and success. But what about it? We have the idea of money but nothing to really explain what it's all about - we don't know if we're getting it, sharing it or even losing it! The idea of Diamonds is not enough by itself - but if we had another card it could shed some light on these notions of money and success.

<u>Action</u>: **Place the Ace of Hearts face up next to the Ace of Diamonds.**

♦♥   That's interesting, the idea of love is also involved. With the focus on money and success but the influence of love this could mean several things such as:

- The money you already own could be better shared amongst friends
- Your current successes could be bettered with family help
- A loved one could help you with your current financial situation
- The luck of a close friend could impact your own life in a positive way

Again, as I tried to make sense of the one concept of finance and success with the influence and dynamic of love, family, partnerships and friends my mind jumped to its own conclusions. I must admit that some came quicker than others, but that is only natural. Sometimes you have to really think about these things before they become apparent and sometimes you have flashes of inspiration.

With only two suits we have learned how the order of cards and concepts is important, and already with just the Hearts and the Diamonds we have a lot of food for thought. This is good - because we want to conjure up as much imagery, ideas and connections as we can when we're looking at the cards - and if we can learn to do this with just two suits then as we expand to the other suits and numbers we're going to be thinking in a creative and useful way from the very start.

```
TOP TIP: THE ORDER OF CARDS IS IMPORTANT AS CARDS SHED LIGHT ON ONE
ANOTHER, EACH CARD REVEALING SOMETHING ABOUT THE CARD BEFORE.
```

Now we're going to move on to the meanings of the black suits of Clubs and Spades, both whose meanings tend to be misunderstood by the average layman.

Clubs and Spades

Unlike the Diamonds and Hearts, Clubs and Spades are less intertwined with today's popular culture and therefore bring with them less built-in meaning. As mentioned earlier, some people may believe that Spades are 'bad' with the Ace of Spades being 'really bad', and most people don't know or haven't even thought about what a Club or a Spade may actually signify. At a push, a Club may be 'something you hit someone on the head with' and a Spade may conjure up images of gardening! Their symbolic relevance has been gradually eroded with time to many people - yet they relate to eternal concepts that are still meaningful to this day.

♣Clubs

If you actually look at the symbol for a Club you'll notice that it doesn't look like the modern interpretation of a Club at all - it certainly doesn't look like a golf club or even a 'caveman club' used for hitting another caveman with. What it DOES look like however is a clover leaf or even a tree, so in some ways we do have the idea of a wooden club. This alone doesn't really get at what the suit of Clubs actually signifies, although it gives us some clues.

A really useful way to imagine what the suit means is in the name itself - CLUB. Not the physical hold-in-your-hand type of club but the idea of a club that you go to or are a member of, a gentleman's club, a nightclub, a social club or the best one of all - a WORKING MAN'S CLUB.

You see the suit of Clubs is all about work, socialising, getting on in life, making things happen, development, growth and living in the 'real world' of commerce, industry and the world around us. And if you think about it, a club in the wooden sense of the word isn't just 'a stick' - it's something that's been crafted and honed into something useful, taken from a tree that grows naturally in the ground. It's the orchard that's been nurtured by a gardener, it's the staff that's been turned by a master craftsman. You get the idea.

Together the idea of social clubs for the upwardly mobile and the concept of crafting things from wood give us the true meaning of the Clubs suit.

- ♣ Work - The day to day 'doing of things' that gets us where we want to go
- ♣ Progress - The idea of growing into something greater than we already are
- ♣ Social - Meetings, partnerships and human interaction
- ♣ Business - Making things happen, learning from some and teaching others

♠ Spades

We come to the fourth and final suit and the one that causes the greatest feelings of dread, panic and outright fear amongst most people. Many folk believe that Spades signify all kinds of bad stuff happening and although Spades are the 'worst' suit in the pack, if we put the Spades into perspective we learn that they're both useful and essential for any card reading.

Before we go any further I want to give you just one sentence to think about:

> **IF YOU DON'T KNOW IT'S COMING YOU CAN'T AVOID IT**

Spades, although dealing mainly with difficulties and obstacles, don't necessarily denote absolute and unavoidable hardship, death or decapitation. The whole point of giving a reading of any kind whether it be with playing cards, Tarot cards or whatever is to present a set of potential outcomes and circumstances which we all have the ability to alter should we choose to pay attention.

Put it this way - if we all believed that fate is set and that a card reading ALWAYS foretold events with one hundred percent accuracy then no one would bother giving themselves or anyone else a reading! If there was no way that I could avoid coming to a rather painful and untimely death involving a revolving door and a bicycle then there would be no point having a reading to foretell this catastrophic future - I'd be better off not knowing about it at all, living the rest of my days in blissful ignorance right up until the point of impact.

The whole point of readings is that fate is in our own hands and life is what we make it. Readings can show us the signs, trends and undercurrents in our lives and allow us a glimpse into many possible futures - yet nothing is cast in stone. Therefore to remove the 'nasty' cards from a reading would actually be doing us, and those we read for, a terrible disservice.

By learning about the potential obstacles in our own future and the futures of others we can make our own choices and act accordingly. And although a reading full of 'nice' cards is something we'd all like to see (we'd all like to have a reading that made us think we were going to win the lottery and meet our perfect lover) it's actually the readings that bring up combinations of ALL the suits, both good and bad, which tend to be the most insightful.

So what does a Spade 'mean' to anyone nowadays? To most of us it is simply the name of a gardening tool, or something you might dig a road with. If we look at the actual symbol of the Spades suit we can see that unlike a spade that we use as a tool, the Spade symbol has a pointed tip rather like a sword. Which is useful, because that pretty much sums it up. As far as we're concerned, it's a sword.

So a Spade represents a sword, but what does that mean? Well, far from being total doom and gloom, the sword represents the battle of everyday life - the struggle, the hardships, the obstacles and the downright bad luck. The sword is a metaphorical weapon and is wielded by all of us as we muddle through our personal wars.

If we can get to grips with these situations, it is up to us to fight the good fight and come out on top. And who wants a story without some epic trials and tribulations anyway? No one - it would be unrealistic. Spades are important because they show us not only where to tread lightly but also when and where to strike. Forewarned is forearmed!

Simply put, the suit of Spades are the obstacles we must face and the trials we must go through if we are to enjoy the benefits of the other suits.

- **Swords** - To be wielded in battle in our everyday struggles
- **Hurdles** - To be seen in advance so we may jump them
- **Obstacles** - That we must clear from our path or sometimes simply avoid
- **Decisions** - That must be made for better or for worse

```
TOP TIP: WHEREAS THE RED CARDS ARE CONSIDERED INHERENTLY 'GOOD', TOO MANY
BLACK CARDS TOGETHER IS SEEN AS 'BAD', EVEN IF ONLY A FEW ARE SPADES.
```

In this next section as before, we're not concerned with what the Aces mean, we're just going to focus on the suits. And once again we're going to imagine that we've just turned over a card in an imaginary reading.

<u>Action</u>: Take out the Ace of Clubs and Ace of Spades from your 'working deck' and write the four descriptions for each suit on each side alongside the four corners of each card as illustrated.

Action: Place the Ace of Clubs face up in front of you.

The club immediately brings to mind business, socialising, working with others and development in our physical lives. But what about it? We have the idea of Clubs, but what's it all about?

Action: Place the Ace of Spades face up next to the Ace of Clubs.

♣♠ With the focus on business, work and socialising but the influence of hurdles and decision making this could mean several things such as:

- A business arrangement could be about to go through a rough patch
- You may have to stand your ground on some work related issues
- Some tough decisions are going to be needed in order to move forward
- You may face some rivalry in your social circle

Again these were the first ideas that sprung to mind with the Club being the focus and the Spade being the influence. Let's try it the other way around and see what happens.

Action: Pick up the Ace of Clubs and the Ace of Spades. Put the Ace of Spades face up in front of you.

Here the focus is firmly on the Spade, the battle and the struggle. This may seem a little more abstract than the other suits when it is the focus - what battle, what struggle? In some ways it can be more internalised - the struggle to get out of bed, to fight our inner demons, to 'get over ourselves' and find the energy to keep going. As I mentioned before, the sword can be wielded yet it can also turn against us in our very hand - we fight ourselves constantly and our worries, anxieties and fears can sometimes get the better of us. The sword is truly double-edged and we either approach it with fear and foreboding or let the fear itself drive us to victory. Some people are ruled by fear. Others are able to harness its power to achieve great things.

Spades are fantastically interesting and the idea that there are continuous battles being fought and won both in our outward lives and innermost thoughts is something you should always bear in mind. A spade can be incredibly revealing and like the opposite suit of Hearts has both an inner and outer emotional relevance whereas the Diamonds and Clubs are almost entirely set in the realm of the practical and real.

Action: Place the Ace of Clubs face up next to the Ace of Spades.

♠♣ With the focus on obstacles and decision making and with the influence of work, the business world and our social circle this could mean:

- Worrying about work is getting in the way of actually doing it
- Our attitude could be having an adverse affect on our job
- We are creating friction at work yet blaming other colleagues
- Business may actually be good but we just can't see it

It's actually quite difficult to come up with things to say when a Spade is the focus - believe me it gets easier when we use more suits and numbers! When a Spade is the focus I tend to talk about personal negativity and lean heavily on the proceeding cards for further insights.

> TOP TIP: AS YOU HAVE FOUR DESCRIPTIONS WRITTEN ON EACH ACE IN YOUR WORKING DECK YOU CAN CREATE DIFFERENT TYPES OF READING BY LOOKING AT DIFFERENT WORDS. TRY DOING A SUIT READING USING ONLY THE WORDS AT THE TOP OF EACH CARD. THEN GIVE THREE OTHER SUIT READINGS USING ONLY THE WORDS ON THE RIGHT, BOTTOM, AND THEN LEFT. THIS WILL HELP YOU COME UP WITH NEW THINGS TO SAY, BUT ALSO START TO HELP YOU UNDERSTAND THE DIFFERENT ASPECTS OF EACH SUIT AND HOW THEY INTERACT WITH EACH OTHER. EVEN AT THIS STAGE AND WITH ONLY FOUR SIMPLE WORDS FOR EACH SUIT, THAT'S A LOT OF DIFFERENT COMBINATIONS!

CHAPTER ONE REVIEW

WE'VE NOW LEARNED WHAT THE FOUR SUITS ACTUALLY MEAN, AND DISCOVERED THAT THE ORDER THEY ARE REVEALED IS VITALLY IMPORTANT FOR OUR UNDERSTANDING.

WE'VE ALSO LEARNED THAT:

DIAMONDS AREN'T JUST ABOUT MONEY BUT ALSO SUCCESS, POWER AND ENERGY

HEARTS AREN'T JUST ABOUT LOVE BUT ALSO FAMILY, EMOTIONS, HEALING AND LUST

CLUBS CAN REFER TO SOCIALISING AND DOING BUSINESS WITH OTHERS

SPADES ARE LIKE SWORDS THAT CAN MAKE US OR BREAK US

REVISION: CHAPTER ONE

1. Can you name three descriptions for the Hearts suit?

2. When we talk about the suit of Clubs, how can we remember what it means?

3. The suit of Spades looks a bit like a garden spade. But what does it really signify?

4. Can you name three descriptions for Diamonds which aren't 'money'?

5. If we call the first card a reading the 'focus', what do we call the second card?

6. Why is the order of cards important?

7. If we dealt a Heart followed by a Diamond, what could we say about that?

8. If we dealt a Club followed by a Spade, what could we say about that?

9. Hearts is simple to remember as 'love'. What else can we say about Hearts?

10. What is so special about the colour of each card? What does it signify?

11. Spades are considered 'scary' by many people. Can you argue against this?

12. Which two suits have an 'inner' and 'outer' meaning and why is that important?

13. What's the easiest way to practice creating readings with your working deck?

13. It can be hard to create a reading when a Spade is first. Why?

14. If we dealt a Diamond followed by a Heart, what could we say about that?

15. If we dealt a Spade followed by a Club, what could we say about that?

16. Does a cartomancy reading tell the future? If not, what does it do?

17. Diamonds aren't just about money but ...., ... and ......?

18. Hearts aren't just about love but also ......, ..., ... and ....?

19. Clubs can refer to socialising and ....?

20. Spades are like .... that can ....?

CHAPTER 2 - PUTTING THE SUITS TOGETHER

So far we've only seen what happens when the red cards or the black cards come after each other. Now we're going to practice the ideas we learned in the last chapter with all four suits together.

<u>Action</u>: Take the four Aces from your working pack (the ones you wrote on in the last chapter) and mix them up face down. Then deal two of these Aces face up in front of you, one next to the other.

Now, you may well be staring at a combination that we've already discussed in the last chapter. If so, try to verbalise OUT LOUD the ideas we have already touched upon. Imagine that you're giving a reading to someone and they're eagerly awaiting your interpretation of the cards. You need to speak, and if you're finding it difficult you need to practice - if you can't talk about a two suit combination you've only just read about in the last chapter I suggest you go back and read it again!

Chances are you're staring at a combination that we haven't yet discussed.

These are:

♦♣	DIAMONDS - CLUBS	♣♥	CLUBS - HEARTS
♣♦	CLUBS - DIAMONDS	♥♠	HEARTS - SPADES
♦♥	DIAMONDS - HEARTS	♠♥	SPADES - HEARTS
♥♦	HEARTS - DIAMONDS	♦♠	DIAMONDS - SPADES
♥♣	HEARTS - CLUBS	♠♦	SPADES - DIAMONDS

You have now learned the concept of how one suit affects another and it's up to you to practice talking the talk with various combinations. You really need to come up with your own ideas about how the suits interact now you've got the idea of it all. You may want to start a notebook detailing your thoughts about each combination as you go. This will enable you to discover which ones you're having problems with and which ones you find the most interesting. You need to <u>practice this process</u> - not learn things by rote.

Just to get you started here are some ideas for a few more examples of suit combinations. A good question to ask yourself as you read these is, why did I write what I did?

♦♣ DIAMONDS + CLUBS

With the focus on money and success, but with the influence of business, work and social life this could mean:

- ❋ Your positive energy may bring work related rewards
- ❋ You should use the money that you do have to bring in new business
- ❋ You're entering a successful and ultimately sociable phase in your life
- ❋ You're in a good position to move things forward rapidly

♥♦   HEARTS + DIAMONDS

With the focus on love, family and relationships, but with the influence of money and success, this could mean:

- A loving partnership may bring unexpected financial rewards
- Following your heart could be the key to success
- You need time to recuperate before you surge back into action
- If you allow yourself some guilty pleasures you may find renewed vigour

♣♥   CLUBS + HEARTS

With the focus on business, work and social life, but with the influence of love, family and relationships, this could mean:

- You need to balance your social life with your home life
- You will find it hard not to mix business with pleasure
- You will get where you want to go with the right person (lover?)
- Progress will be made, but it may be an emotional ride

Please use these ideas as a springboard and where possible come up with as many of your own ideas as you can. Keep mixing the cards up and doing dummy readings just with the suits, keep talking out loud, and see how MUCH you can say about a combination, even if you get stuck and really have to think! The more you do it, the easier it will get.

Use the Aces from your working pack, and then use the Aces from your normal pack. What you really want to aim for is being able to do these suit only readings using the normal pack without the memory aids. If you find this a bit tricky, go back and read each section on the suits again. The better image you can create in your mind of each suit the easier they will be to remember.

The fact that you've written four words on each of the working cards means that the orientation of the cards can sometimes mean there is a different word at the top of each card. Mix the cards up sideways and lengthways when you're practicing these simple readings, and use different words from each card to come up with different things to say.

When you move to using a normal deck you'll be left with the essence of all four words for each card in your mind and should be able to conjure up all kinds of possibilities and outcomes for yourself or someone else.

PRACTICING THE SUITS

You need to practice talking about suit combinations until you're fairly confident with them. Spend time shuffling the four Aces and dealing two cards face up in front of you, and then extemporising OUT LOUD on what you see. You CANNOT learn without speaking out loud - keeping your thoughts to yourself about what each card means will not get you anywhere. You need to practice EXPLAINING what you see, as if someone else was there. Trust me, if you do it now and keep doing it while you're learning, giving your first reading for someone will be an enjoyable experience instead of an embarrassing silence.

First use the four Aces from your working pack. When you feel like you're gaining in confidence, switch to the four unmarked Aces from your normal pack. You may feel a bit lost at first without the words to guide you, but with a bit of practice you may find the lack of words quite liberating and you may be surprised what you come up with as you stumble over your words trying to make sense of it all!

CHAPTER TWO REVIEW

THIS CHAPTER IS ALL ABOUT PRACTICING SUIT COMBINATIONS AND LEARNING TO COME UP WITH YOUR OWN WORDS TO DESCRIBE THEM

WE KNOW THAT THE FIRST CARD DRAWN IS ALWAYS THE FOCUS AND THE NEXT CARD IS THE INFLUENCE ON THAT FIRST CARD

WE HAVE TALKED ABOUT SEVERAL SETS OF CARDS AND HOW TO APPROACH A TWO CARD READING - YOU MUST START WORKING OUT THESE TWO CARD COMBINATIONS FOR YOURSELF

ALTHOUGH WE HAVE WRITTEN ON SOME OF THE CARDS, YOU MAY WANT TO GRAB A NOTEBOOK FOR SOME NOTES AS YOU GO, AND YOU MAY FIND IT USEFUL TO WRITE DOWN ANY INTERESTING OR CHALLENGING TWO-SUIT COMBINATIONS AS THEY OCCUR TO YOU

WE HAVE TOUCHED ON SPADES/CLUBS, CLUBS/SPADES, HEARTS/DIAMONDS, DIAMONDS/HEARTS, DIAMONDS/CLUBS AND CLUBS/HEARTS.

MAKE SURE YOU UNDERSTAND HOW THESE EXAMPLES ACTUALLY WORK AND REFER TO THEM SHOULD YOU GET A BIT STUCK

```
TOP TIP:

IF YOU'RE HAVING PROBLEMS REMEMBERING THE SUITS, HERE'S A GOOD WAY OF
GETTING YOUR BRAIN IN GEAR BY SORTING THROUGH SOME IDEAS USING A MIND-
MAP:

1. WRITE THE NAME OF A SUIT YOU'RE FINDING HARD TO REMEMBER OR RELATE TO
IN THE CENTRE OF A SHEET OF PAPER

2. TRY AND WRITE AS MANY CONCEPTS AND IDEAS YOU CAN THINK OF THAT CONNECT
TO THE SUIT AS YOU CAN, LINKING EACH ONE WITH A LINE TO THE SUIT NAME

3. IF YOU HAVE NEW IDEAS THAT OFFSHOOT FROM YOUR INITIAL IDEAS,
KEEP GOING AND SEE WHERE THEY TAKE YOU - MAKE THE MIND MAP AS BIG AS YOU
CAN AND DON'T BE AFRAID TO HAVE STRANGE AND OFTEN IRRELEVANT IDEAS!

MAKE A MIND MAP FOR ALL FOUR SUITS - WHICH DID YOU FIND EASIEST TO
CREATE? WHICH DID YOU FIND THE HARDEST AND WHY? WORK ON THE SUITS YOU
DON'T QUITE 'GET' WITH THIS METHOD UNTIL YOU FEEL MORE COMFORTABLE WITH
THEM.
```

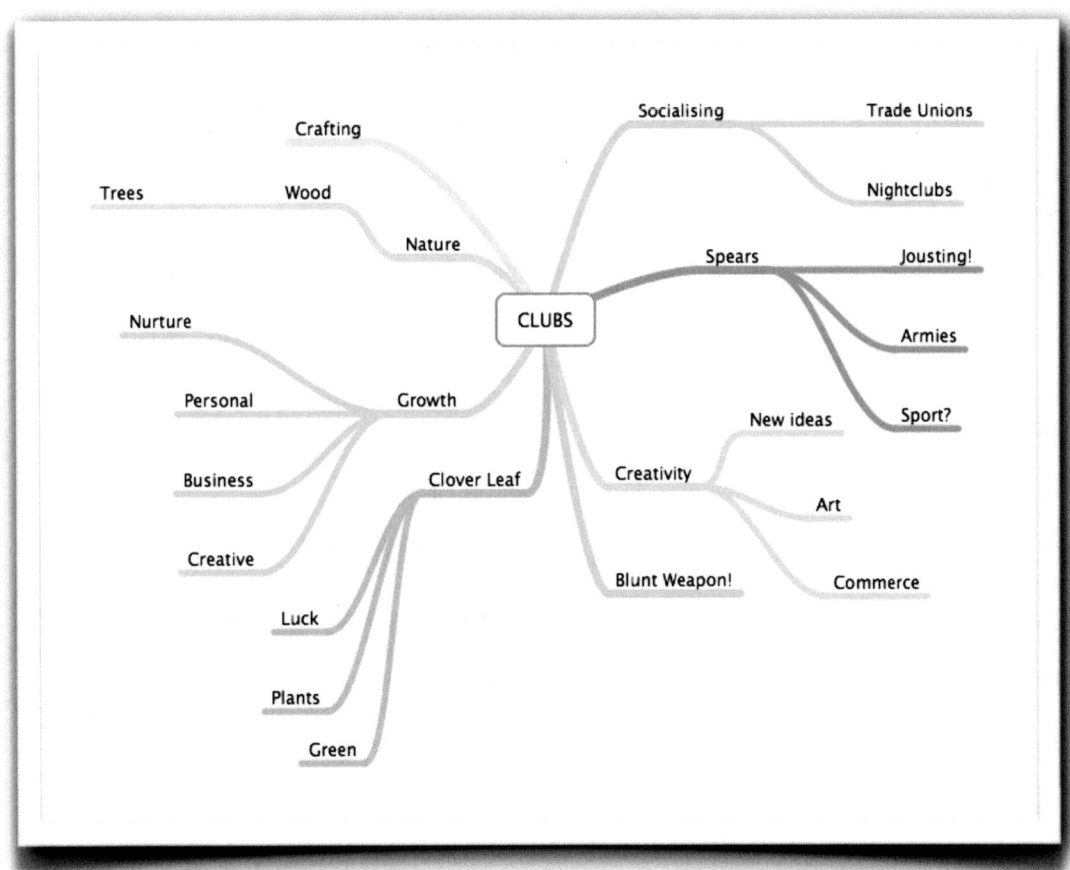

**A very rough mind-map based around clubs - try and make your own up for each suit
and see where your ideas take you, no matter how crazy! Try and make each mind
map as large as you can and write anything that comes to mind.**

REVISION: CHAPTER TWO

1. What could you say about a Diamond followed by a Club?

2. What's the best way to practice giving two-suit readings?

3. If you're unsure about the meaning of a particular suit, what's a good way to go?

4. You lay out a Club followed by a Heart. What could that mean?

5. How many combinations of two suits can you get?

6. The second card we lay down is the 'influence' on the first card, called what?

7. What's a good way to practice using the words on the cards?

8. What could you say about a Spade following a Diamond?

9. What could you say about a Heart followed by a Club?

10. You lay down a Diamond followed by a Spade. What could that mean?

11. It hasn't been discussed yet, but what could it mean if a Heart followed a Heart?

12. Explain the difference between a Club following a Diamond, as opposed to a Diamond following a Club.

13. If a Heart followed a Spade, what kinds of influences are being brought to the Spade?

14. If a Diamond followed a Heart, what influences are being brought to the Heart?

15. If someone asked you what the suit of Spades actually signified, what would you tell them?

16. What's the difference between a Diamond and a Club?

17. How many words can you use to describe the suit of Hearts?

18. How many words can you use to describe the Diamonds suit. Is it more than Hearts?

19. Which suit do you find it easier to describe - Clubs or Spades? Why?

20. Imagine you drop a pack of cards on the floor and see two suits. Give an immediate 'reading' about those two cards, out loud - right now! Can you do it?

CHAPTER 3 - THREE CARD SUIT READINGS

The basic system for giving cartomancy readings is based on three cards. As we've learned, the order that cards are revealed is important, and when you turn over three cards this is also true. However, when you deal three cards face up for a cartomancy reading, the second card is the influence of the first card, and the third card is the influence on the second card!

Using this idea we can get some concept of time and progression - three cards can show us how things are going and where they're headed. Some people use a simple past - present - future reading for the three cards, and although this isn't far off the idea it is missing the point somewhat.

When you understand how one card affects the meaning of the card before it the order of the cards takes on a deeper meaning and their combinations are far more related than taking each card at face value and assigning it a time slot. With this relational system we get more of a feel of the current trends taking place, as opposed to a reading that states 'this happened to you in the past' and 'this card is your future'. We want to avoid that way of thinking altogether as it simply doesn't give us enough scope to see the bigger picture.

So using what we've already learned it's not hard to see how this type of reading could progress. You simply lay out three cards face up in a row and read the cards together, just like we did with two cards.

Action: **Shuffle up the four Aces from your working pack face down. Then deal three of them face up alongside each other.**

You now have three Aces staring up at you. We start at the left like before, this first card being the focus and the second card being the influence. When we have given this some thought and discussed what it could mean we move on to the second card as the focus and the third card as the influence.

So we are simply doing a two card reading twice! The middle card influences the first card, that in turn is influenced by the third card.

Colour readings

Before you do anything however, a good way to get a quick overview of a reading is to go one step *simpler* and think of the red cards as good and black cards as bad. For instance:

BLACK BLACK RED

Things have been tough but are going to get better in the future

RED RED BLACK

It's been plain sailing so far, but look out for clouds on the horizon

RED BLACK RED

You're entering a rough patch but things will get better

BLACK RED BLACK

Things have taken a turn for the better, but it's not over yet

Although this is rather simplistic it can give you a very quick feel for a three card reading and it's a good way of making sure you're thinking in the right way about the cards and their order before you open your mouth.

<u>Action</u>: Spend some time giving yourself or an imaginary friend some suit readings like this incorporating the colour method, each time mixing the Aces up again and laying three cards out in front of you.

Here are a few examples, which include the overall 'colour' reading in brackets:

♣♠♦ **Clubs Spades** Diamonds *(Things have been tough but going to get better)*

- Your job could be about to go through a rough patch associated with some kind of power struggle - however you will come out on top
- Progress is difficult and it seems many time consuming hurdles will be placed in your way, yet you will find the energy to overcome them
- Certain people in certain circles are looking to block you financially, but you'll get your way eventually
- Business deals seemed wracked by indecision - however this arduous process will ultimately lead to success

♥♦♣ **Hearts Diamonds Clubs** *(Plain sailing so far, look out for clouds on the horizon)*

- A partnership could soon be forged with a powerful person at work - you should however tread with caution
- You will be going through an emotional yet energy filled period which will ultimately end up with progress being made - but take care not to burn out
- You need to spend some 'me' time and spend a little money on yourself, and perhaps go on holiday or start getting out more
- You can begin to start enjoying yourself a little more as things turn in your favour regarding business - but don't let your guard down

♥♠♦ **Hearts Spades** Diamonds *(You're entering a rough patch but things will get better)*

- A relationship could be put under intense pressure due to money related worries although this will be resolved
- Emotions will run high as you overcome some obstacles with great success
- Although there is little time to charge your batteries at present, you will find the inner strength to carry on to happier times
- You need to decide what really makes you happy, but need to actually put some thought into it, which will in itself make you a lot happier!

As you practice giving yourself these three card readings you will gradually begin to see patterns and meaning in the cards at a glance - an 'overview' of the situation. This is extremely useful and is something you should definitely work on developing.

The colour reading gives you an instant framework in which to set the reading and is extremely valuable, even though it's so simple. It enables you to get an instant grip on the shape of the reading, making deciphering the cards that much easier. Instead of looking at the first two cards and wondering what to say, the fact that you can get an immediate overview of 'where it's all going' can help put you at ease before you start.

<u>Action</u>: **We're about to move on to the spot cards. Before we do that, and when you are somewhat comfortable giving suit readings, you should write the suit meanings on ALL of the spot cards. It could take a while, but at the very least it will hammer home the meanings of the suits!**

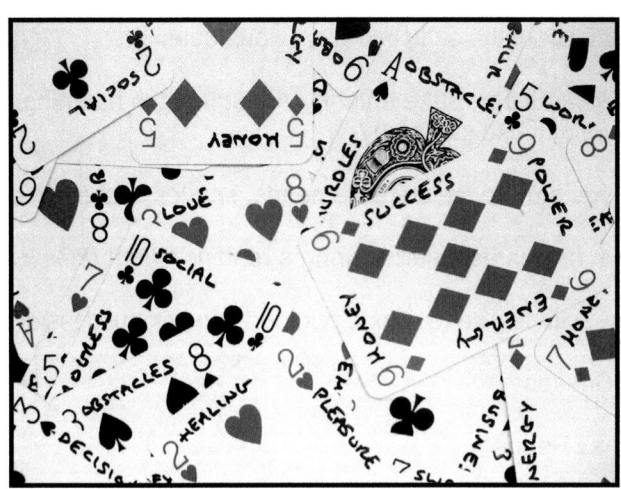

CHAPTER THREE REVIEW

WE'VE DISCUSSED IN SOME DETAIL THE MEANINGS OF THE SUITS AND HOW THEY INTERACT WITH EACH OTHER. HOPEFULLY BY THIS POINT YOU HAVE A SOLID UNDERSTANDING OF THE SUIT MEANINGS THAT IS VITAL BEFORE YOU BEGIN TO CONNECT THE SUITS TO THEIR NUMBER VALUES.

IF YOU STILL DON'T FEEL ENTIRELY COMFORTABLE WITH GIVING SUIT READINGS I RECOMMEND YOU GO BACK AND RE-READ THE LAST FEW CHAPTERS. THERE'S NO POINT GOING ON UNTIL YOU'VE GOT THE SUITS FIRMLY FIXED IN YOUR MIND.

KEEP PRACTICING WITH THE WORKING DECK AND THE NORMAL DECK UNTIL YOU'RE AT LEAST ABLE TO STRING SOME SENTENCES TOGETHER AND GENERALLY 'MAKE SENSE' WHEN YOU SEE CARD COMBINATIONS.

QUESTIONS : CHAPTER THREE

1. What's the difference between a two card reading and a three card reading?

2. The three cards in a three card reading could be seen as past, present and future. But what could be a better way of approaching these cards?

3. How can the colours of the cards help us?

4. If you saw two black cards followed by a red card, what could you say about that?

5. If you dealt out two red cards followed by a black card, what could that mean?

6. You lay out a club, spade and a diamond. Using just the colours, what could that mean?

7. What could you say about the suits in the previous question?

8. If I described three cards as 'You're entering a rough patch but things will get better', what could the colours of these cards be?

9. During a reading you turn up the suits diamonds, spades, clubs. What could you say?

10. You turn up clubs, diamonds, hearts during a reading. What does it mean?

For these next ten questions give readings out loud in quick succession for each set:

11. Clubs / Hearts / Spades

12. Diamonds / Clubs / Hearts

13. Clubs / Diamonds / Spades

14. Hearts / Spades / Clubs

15. Spades / Clubs / Diamonds

16. Diamonds / Hearts / Spades

17. Clubs / Spades / Hearts

18. Diamonds / Spades / Hearts

19. Clubs / Hearts / Diamonds

20. Spades / Hearts / Clubs

CHAPTER 4 - THE SPOT CARDS

The numbers one to ten each have their own significance yet for many people remembering what they each signify can be a real chore - numbers can appear abstract and devoid of meaning and on their own they aren't particularly evocative.

When we talk about Hearts, Diamonds, Clubs and Spades we conjure up concepts that we understand and the visual aspect of these suits helps us do this - the suits actually look and feel like 'things' we're used to talking about. Numbers are largely abstract to most people and don't conjure up images of anything.

We need to learn to get 'visual' with our numbers and aim to connect as much meaning to them as possible. When you see a number you need a whole array of ideas, concepts and images to come to mind, just as they do with the four suits.

If you know nothing about numerology then it's probably the case that when you see a number it's just that - a number. We need to get creative with our visualising so we can actually learn, with practice, what the numbers mean.

Here are the basic meanings of the numbers one through ten*:

1. **Beginnings**
2. **Cooperation**
3. **Expansion**
4. **Security**
5. **Activity**
6. **Communication**
7. **Spirituality**
8. **Inspiration**
9. **Changes**
10. **Success**

> ** You may already know something about numerology or have your own system of remembering what the numbers mean. The descriptions in this chapter and in the rest of this book, although simplified to make things easier to learn, do adhere to the commonly accepted numerology meanings for each number.*

The numbers one to ten go through a cycle and the 10 at the end is in many ways similar to the 1 at the start - the 10 is the realisation of all that the 1 can be. If you think of all the numbers going around in a big circle starting and ending on the 1 like a clock you get the idea - the ten becomes a one again and the cycle repeats. This is analogous to the 'life cycle' that we all go through.

Think about this little story for a moment. We all begin alone (1) we couple up (2) and bring life into the world (3) before we make a home with four walls (4). There is much activity as the child grows (5) and before long the child learns to communicate (6) and ask big questions about the world around him (7). Finally he is inspired to go out into the world (8) make a difference (9) and be successful (10). He's now alone (1) and the cycle can begin again.

By thinking of the numbers in this way it also gives us the feeling of progression - higher numbers are the end of the cycle and lower numbers the start of the cycle. This is very useful in readings.

Let me go through that story again in greater detail. This whole story is designed so that you can remember the meanings of the numbers quickly and easily.

1 THE POWER OF ONE

I STAND ALONE

We have to start somewhere, and with a blank canvas there is a lot of energy and optimism. We could be starting from scratch, or starting again (coming full circle). We're number one! There's no fear - anything's possible. This number one isn't about knowing you've arrived - it's about knowing you could get there if you put your mind to it. It's the optimism and naivety of a teenager who's willing to try anything and is free from old habits or preconceived notions. This number one is selfish - but's it's a healthy selfish - not the kind that crushes other people but drags others along with it's sheer optimism and idealistic outlook. Powerful stuff! However this boundless energy can be lacking in direction somewhat - it needs focus to be truly effective.

Memory Tip: The number 1 looks like a capital I

2 ME AND YOU

TWO'S COMPANY

We don't stay alone and single forever. We meet someone, fall in love and in many ways our ego takes a step back as we learn to care for someone else. We learn to share, we learn to cooperate and do things together as a team. It's not always easy but it brings great rewards. We get to see the world another way, and we also learn to see things from another point of view. We form partnerships not just in our personal lives but our professional lives too.

*Memory Tip: A number 2 looking in the mirror to it's left creates a heart shape
You can also imagine this as two swans coming together to create a heart silhouette*

3 WE CREATE LIFE

THREE'S A CROWD

Only two people can bring a third person into the world - it's how the human race has expanded to cover the entire globe. It's the growth of something from nothing, the fruits of cooperation. There can be labour pains, but the rewards are great. Let's not forget that even business partners often refer to their companies as 'babies' - the number three is all to do with seeing things come to life and grow beyond a mere concept.

Memory Tip: The number 3 looks like a pair of breasts to feed a baby

4 WE MAKE A HOME

THESE FOUR WALLS

When a child enters a couple's life they seek stability and the four walls of a place they can call 'home' for their family. Structure and order are required, safety and practicality. Although a lot needs to be done, there is a sense of settling down combined with achievement. For many people this is the end of a cycle for them as a happy home life with children is one of their life goals. Kids or not, the four represents the solid foundation required for future plans and growth.

Memory Tip: A square has four sides, like a simplistic house shape with square windows and doors

5 THE FAMILY GROWS

FIVE ALIVE

Once a baby becomes a child things get pretty hectic - a hive of activity! There's always something to do, plans to make - life is certainly never the same again. Life seems to go at twice the speed, everything seems to happen at once and multi-tasking is the order of the day. There is growth in so many ways - physically, mentally and socially - and sometimes it can feel out of control. One thing's for sure - you can't halt progress. This isn't like the number 3 which creates something from nothing - this is the growth of things that are already there.

Memory Tip: The number 5 looks like the handlebars and front wheel of a kids scooter which can remind you of the notion of speed and movement

6 THE CHILD LEARNS TO COMMUNICATE

SIX IS SOCIAL

Before long the child is starting to communicate with the world around him and it's about personal interaction and a need to be understood. A child may attempt to communicate with sounds, looks and actions - even with his building blocks! The number six isn't just about phoning people up, it's about connecting with people too.

Memory Tip: The number 6 looks like an eye, or an ear, or a telephone

7 THE CHILD ASKS BIG QUESTIONS

SEVENTH HEAVEN

Once the child has learned to communicate he can start asking questions - and quite quickly they're questions we can hardly answer. 'Where did I come from?' is always a good one - it's funny how some of the first questions we ask as children are so difficult to answer! This need to understand and ask big questions has a spiritual ring to it - where did we come from, how did we get here, what's it all about? The seven is all about looking up to the stars as we ask for some kind of divine inspiration.

Memory Tip: The number 7 looks like a question mark

---

8 THE CHILD IS INSPIRED TO LEAVE HOME

EIGHT THROUGH THE GATE

The eight is when you leave home and do it for yourself, make your first strides towards independence and try out some of your own ideas for a change. You've got to get out there and make things happen, but it takes a leap of faith. You've got to believe you're ready for it but it takes inspiration and personal belief. It's almost like that lightbulb over the head moment where you 'get it' or have some flash of inspiration. But it's also about making the leap of faith required to make it happen.

Memory Tip: The number 8 looks like two 3's put together side on - the number 3 is the child, the number 8 being twice his size and ready to move on

---

9 HE MAKES A DIFFERENCE

PLAN NINE (FROM OUTER SPACE)

You go out into the world and try to make a difference - you try and enable change. Unless things change you can very rarely get to where you want to go. Some of these changes will be changes you have to go through yourself, but many of them will be the changes which you've pushed through to reach your ultimate goal - indeed there may well be sacrifices. When you can almost smell success you can't let anything get in your way and have to at times be ruthless. Nine is about nearly having it all. Don't give up - everything's going the right way.

Memory Tip: The number 9 is the activity before the success of 10/10
Like 6, the number 9 also looks like eye, ear, telephone but this time it's on a higher more adult level of communication and action fuelled by determination and knowledge

10 HE BECOMES SUCCESSFUL

TEN OUT OF TEN

The child has realised his dreams and in many ways he has grown up. He has made a success of himself and achieved his ambitions. There is a sense of finality and accomplishment and the end of a cycle. The ten is for top marks, abundance and accomplishments earned through hard work - it took all the other stages to reach this point. With this sense of accomplishment can also come the sense of looking for pastures new - for another challenge. There can be a big difference between success and stability.

Memory Tip: Top marks, the realisation of a goal or dream
The end of a cycle and the start of a new one

This is just one way of looking at the numbers one to ten, but I wanted to explain the life cycle idea first because it's one of the easiest to remember. Some of the numbers are easier to grasp than others so here are some other things to bear in mind when you're trying to remember all of this:

1 and **10** are obviously beginnings and endings - the starts of things and everything that's exciting about new ventures, and the ends of things and the satisfaction of completion

2 for cooperation is pretty easy to remember, for love, balance, coming together

3 for expansion makes sense when you think of two people having a third to create a family - it's about concepts becoming reality and partnerships bearing fruit

4 for stability makes sense when you think of the four walls of a house - the family need somewhere to live, solid foundations

5 for the growth in the home itself, and the 'hive' of activity inside needing to expand outside of the four walls - it's the four walls of the house, with something growing inside of it!

6 for communication, the 6 looks like an eye, an ear AND a telephone!

7 for the spiritual 'seventh heaven' and the questioning shape like a question mark

8 is 'out of the gate' - getting out there and doing it

9 is the final push for victory, the last mile, the planning coming to fruition

10 is the successful outcome, the realisation of everything that has gone before, the end of one cycle and the start of another

LET'S REMIND OURSELVES OF THE WHOLE STORY ANOTHER WAY, THIS TIME DIVIDING THE NUMBERS INTO THREE 'CHAPTERS' OR SECTIONS:

1-3 : I STAND ALONE / TWO'S COMPANY / THREE'S A CROWD

The first three numbers are about fresh starts and early development

The numbers 1-3 have their own little story. A single person (1) meets someone (2) and has a baby (3). When you're a single young adult (1) it's all about excitement and trying new things out with great enthusiasm. Then you meet someone (2) and share your life with them in a less selfish way. Then (sometimes!) you have a baby (3) and you've both made a new number one!

These first three numbers are relatively easy to understand. I Stand Alone, Two's Company & Three's A Crowd are well known sayings and perfectly illustrate what each number means.

4-7 : FOUR WALLS / FIVE ALIVE / SIX IS SOCIAL / 7TH HEAVEN

Numbers four to seven are more to do with childhood and the family growing

Security is needed so a house (4) is built for the family to live in. The baby grows into a child (5) and introduces all that crazy activity that revolves around having kids. The child learns to communicate and becomes a true member of the family (6). As he becomes a young adult he asks more big questions and becomes more aware of his place in the world (7).

8-10 : EIGHT THROUGH THE GATE / PLAN NINE / TEN OUT OF TEN

These last numbers are more to do with adulthood and achievement

Finally the young adult leaves home to go and make his way in the world (8). He makes things happen, and his involvement in the real world shapes that world, even changes it (9). He becomes successful, realises his dreams and is able to stand on his own two feet (10). The moment this happens however the cycle is over and it is now HE who is the number one.

Action: Go through each of the spot cards in your working deck, writing the one word meanings of each number on each card. You can do this in the centre of each card, or along the side - wherever you can find space! It gets harder for the higher numbers as there's less space to write on so don't worry about it looking too perfect!

CHAPTER FOUR REVIEW

IT CAN BE QUITE TRICKY TO GET THE MEANINGS OF THE NUMBERS ONE TO TEN FIRMLY STUCK IN YOUR HEAD. DON'T BE TOO WORRIED IF YOU CAN'T IMMEDIATELY REMEMBER THE MEANINGS OF ALL THE NUMBERS - IT CAN TAKE A WHILE FOR IT ALL TO SINK IN.

IF YOU'RE FINDING IT HARD, TRY TAKING ONE SUIT OF THE SPOT CARDS FROM A DECK, AND SEE IF YOU CAN DESCRIBE EACH NUMBER ONE AT A TIME IN ORDER. THEN MIX THEM UP AND TEST YOURSELF RANDOMLY AND IDENTIFY WHICH NUMBERS YOU'RE HAVING THE MOST PROBLEMS WITH.

SOME OF THE NUMBERS WILL BE MUCH EASIER THAN THE OTHERS TO REMEMBER. FOR INSTANCE, IT'S USUALLY EASIER TO REMEMBER THE FIRST FEW NUMBERS AND THE LAST FEW NUMBERS. IF YOU CAN BE HONEST WITH YOURSELF ABOUT WHICH NUMBERS YOU'RE HAVING PROBLEMS WITH YOU CAN REVISE THE 'DIFFICULT' NUMBERS VERY QUICKLY.

REVISION: CHAPTER FOUR

1. Can you describe what the numbers ten and one signify? How are they similar?

2. What common phrase could help you remember the meaning of the number three?

3. The number six looks like a few things that could help you remember it. What are they?

4. Seven rhymes with what? What do the sevens in the deck mean?

5. One of the numbers is all about love, families and partnerships. Which one?

6. What's the difference between the number five and the number three? How are they similar?

7. How many things about the number four could you say relate to its actual meaning?

8. Of all the numbers, which would you say were the 'best'? Why?

9. What's the difference between the number eight and the number five? How are they similar?

10. If you were about to achieve great success at home, which two numbers could you use to describe that outcome?

11. If you were about to find some kind of spiritual love, which two numbers could you use to describe that outcome?

12. Can you name two numbers that together could mean new starts based on communication?

13. If I was talking about the growth of new things from ideas, which one number could I be referring to?

14. Talking out loud, give a short description of each even number between one and ten.

15. Talking out loud, give a short description of each odd number between one and ten.

16. 'I can see from these numbers that there is romance in the air, and things are moving quickly to a fortunate conclusion'. Which two numbers could I be talking about?

17. 'Your mind seems to be on higher things, but in fact you need to focus more on your home life'. Which two numbers could I be talking about?

18. 'This is a time of things taking shape from some of your ideas. This new-found energy will bring you new friends and help you communicate your ideas with others.' How many numbers could I have been talking about in that sentence and which ones?

19. Finish these phrases: '..... through the gate' - '....... heaven' - '... to tango'

20 Finish these phrases: '. ..... alone' - '.... company' - '... out of ...' - '...... a crowd'

CHAPTER 5 - DECIPHERING THE SPOT CARDS

We have now covered what the four suits and the spot cards one to ten mean. We are now in a position to learn what all forty spot cards in the pack mean. The good news is, because we've learnt the meanings of the suits and the meanings of the numbers independently from each other, we don't so much have to learn each card by rote but can simply 'read' each card in a similar way to how we practiced giving suit-only readings.

Simply put, we 'read' a card by taking the number idea (the focus) with the influence of the suit idea (the influence). We have four key words to describe each suit so each card could mean a variety of slightly different things. For now, lets just choose one keyword for each suit, and apply them to a few cards.

Here are some brief examples, using only one aspect of each suit:

6♣ **SIX OF CLUBS (USING THE KEYWORD 'COMMUNICATION')**

We know that a six is all about communication. But with the influence of Clubs (which are about socialising and work) we know that this combination means that one of the meanings of the Six Of Clubs is communication in the workplace.

9♦ **NINE OF DIAMONDS (USING THE KEYWORD 'SUCCESS')**

We know that a nine is about things coming to fruition, and with the influence of Diamonds (signifying money and energy) we know that this combination means that one of the meanings of the Nine Of Diamonds is a fortuitous financial and successful card.

7♠ **SEVEN OF SPADES (USING THE KEYWORD 'OBSTACLES')**

We know that a seven is about higher more spiritual things, and with the Spades influence of conflict and obstacles we can assume that one of the meanings of the Seven Of Spades is to do with conflicts of a more internal and spiritual nature, for instance a loss of nerve perhaps or a lack of faith.

4♥ **FOUR OF HEARTS (USING THE KEYWORD 'LOVE')**

We know that a four is to do with stability and security, and with the Hearts influence of love we get the idea that one of the meanings of the Four Of Hearts could be to do with a strong and deep love that comes through understanding and working at things together.

As you can see, by knowing the meanings of the suits and the numbers it is possible to 'read' just one card to find out the whole card's meaning. This is the key to quickly understanding what each of the forty spot cards mean. Of course in the four examples given above we have taken just one keyword or idea from each suit and coupled it with each number. This is a fairly two dimensional way to view each card however - with four keywords each spot card has a variety of slightly different meanings, and of course the keywords are only there to help you quickly grasp each suit. In actual fact the possibilities for each card are far greater.

It is at this point that you may begin to understand and come to terms with the huge amount of information contained in each card. This is a good thing, as it means you won't be short of words when you start to give readings!

<u>Action</u>: **Go through all the spot cards in your normal pack 'reading' each card carefully as you go to come to an understanding of each card's true meaning. Take your time and think about each card. Some cards will be easier than others.**

After having gone through the pack myself, here are some cards that for some reason jumped out at me as especially strong:

3♦   THREE OF DIAMONDS

With the expansion and new creation of the three, and the power and success of diamonds, this card really stands out as a card showing new ventures taking shape.

9♦   NINE OF DIAMONDS

With the dynamic nine signifying things moving rapidly and successfully in the right direction with a current project, and the financial success of diamonds, this card is extremely fortuitous and shows the rapid and rewarding developments of existing undertakings.

10♦   TEN OF DIAMONDS

Signifying the successful completion of a project or existing life cycle, with the rewards and power of diamonds, this is a tremendously auspicious card. Like all tens, it is about completion and therefore the end of one cycle and start of another.

5♣   FIVE OF CLUBS

With the organic growth of the five with the work aspect of clubs, this card brings to mind the idea of things really taking shape at work - from solid foundations things are really starting to grow and develop.

9♣   NINE OF CLUBS

With the nine signifying things coming to fruition, and the social and work aspects of clubs, this card is a strong indicator of work plans coming together and social engagements taking a front seat.

10♣   TEN OF CLUBS

With the end of a cycle and the goals being reached, with the work ethic of clubs, it's no surprise that this is possibly one of the best work related cards in the deck, the completion of long term projects and successful ventures.

2♥   **TWO OF HEARTS**

We know that the two is about partnerships and sharing, and with the Hearts influence, also about love and pleasure, it is no surprise to find that the two of hearts is one of the most romantic cards in the pack and is a strong indicator of good relationships and happy marriages.

3♥   **THREE OF HEARTS**

With the idea of partnerships bearing fruit, and the love and romance aspect of hearts, this card can't help but be a romantic card but with the added possibility of love turning into much more - a child on the horizon perhaps? Or if not romance, the development of partnerships into fruitful relationships that go much deeper.

7♥   **SEVEN OF HEARTS**

With the mystical and higher thinking seven, and the love aspect of hearts, this is a very spiritual card and can mean a breakthrough in all things spiritual, or of pure matters of the heart and soul - the kind of happiness that can only come from within - or above!

9♠   **NINE OF SPADES**

With nine signifying great movement near the end of a project and the spades signifying obstacles, this card shows that the last few steps of a current endeavour may well be extremely challenging and one should look out for last minute snags and surprises.

10♠   **TEN OF SPADES**

With the ten being all about the successful completion of goals, yet spades signifying hurdles and fights, this card is possibly the most conflicted in the deck. As it stands, it is quite hard to read this card alone and care must be taken to see this card in context with the rest of the reading. One positive aspect of this card is that the ten is the end of a cycle and that after times of great upheaval comes the chance to start anew.

A♦♣♥♠ **THE FOUR ACES**

The Aces are all about the energy of starting - of raw drive and will. Consequently they 'energise' the suits that they are coupled with. The Ace of Diamonds is about the pure force of money and power, the Ace of Clubs is all about the strength and determination of work and growth, the Ace of Hearts is the essence of love and emotions, and the Ace of Spades is the power of the warrior to take on anything. These cards are somewhat naive - they are the raw power of each suit before steps have been taken - and as such they effect all the cards around them with their idealistic and unquestioned power.

Action: Go through your working deck, once again reading each card. As you have ideas, write them on the card faces. Try and get at least one extra word and phrase on each card - two if possible. This will get your brain in gear, and also make you realise which cards you understand the best and which cards you don't instantly 'get'. Some of your ideas may be quite specific such as 'Communication at work'. Other times you may get a vague notion for a card and write on the card anyway. The important thing is that you think about each card and write down anything you think is interesting on the cards themselves as this will greatly speed up the learning process.

```
            CHAPTER FIVE REVIEW

    YOU CAN DECIPHER ANY SPOT CARD MEANING BY SIMPLY
         ATTACHING THE MEANING OF THE NUMBER TO
                THE MEANING OF THE SUIT

   AS THERE ARE SEVERAL MEANINGS OR ASPECTS TO EACH SUIT,
       THIS GIVES EACH SPOT CARD A VARIETY OF MEANINGS

    ALTHOUGH YOU CAN USE THE NUMBER AS THE FOCUS AND THE
  SUIT AS THE INFLUENCE, DECIPHERING A CARD IS MORE OF A
     TWO WAY STREET - TRY USING THE SUIT AS THE FOCUS AND
    THE NUMBER AS THE INFLUENCE FOR A DIFFERENT VIEWPOINT

    YOU SHOULD BE ABLE TO GO THROUGH ALL FORTY SPOT CARDS
   IN A DECK AND COME UP WITH SOMETHING TO SAY ABOUT THEM
    - SINGLE OUT THE CARDS YOU ARE STRUGGLING WITH AND FIX
     THEM IN YOUR MIND BY ADDING MORE WORDS TO THESE CARDS
```

REVISION: CHAPTER FIVE

1. Which card is possibly the most difficult and conflicted card in the deck? Why?

2. If you had to pick the most spiritual card from the spot cards, which would it be?

3. Explain which card is the most likely to concern the completion of work projects.

4. 'This card represents ventures and financial matters taking shape'. Which card is it?

5. There's one card that can show last minute snags and hurdles which is called what?

6. There are two 'love' cards that deal with coming together, and then developing that love into something new and possibly the tiny patter of feet! Which two cards are they?

7. If I told you that things were starting to take shape at work from solid foundations, which card could I be talking about?

8. Explain what the four aces are all about, and then elaborate on each individual ace.

9. One card in the deck more than any could mean a financial windfall. Which is it?

10. If a card told you a work project was finally coming to fruition, which card could it be?

11. I am all about hearing about some good financial news. Which card am I?

12. I'm all about family matters coming to a head in a good way. Which card am I?

13. I'm all about finding it tough to get things moving. Which card am I?

14. I'm a card that deals with a real sense of personal fulfilment at work. Which card am I?

15. I'm a card that could indicate the power of love in your life. Which card am I?

16. If I was to say 'homebuilding', which card should spring to mind?

17. I am thinking about a card that could indicate problems with relationships. Which is it?

18. This card indicates a potential business partnership. What's it called?

19. I'm a card of financial rewards based on a strong foundation. What card am I?

20. A family or romantic cycle is complete in all the best ways possible. Which card am I talking about?

REVISION STOP: CHAPTERS ONE TO FIVE

YOU SHOULD HAVE NOW LEARNT

SUIT MEANINGS

SUIT INTERACTIONS

SUIT ONLY READINGS

NUMBER (NUMEROLOGY) MEANINGS

HOW TO DECIPHER THE SPOT CARDS

THE SPOT CARD MEANINGS

YOU SHOULD NOW OWN

A DECK OF CARDS WHOSE SPOT CARDS ARE ALL WRITTEN ON WITH THEIR SUIT AND NUMBER MEANINGS

ALSO

YOU SHOULD HAVE ALSO SCRIBBLED YOUR OWN IDEAS ON THEM TOO!

CAN YOU ANSWER EVERY REVISION QUESTION EASILY?

REVISION CHAPTER ONE PAGE FIFTEEN
REVISION CHAPTER TWO PAGE TWENTY
REVISION CHAPTER THREE PAGE TWENTY FOUR
REVISION CHAPTER FOUR PAGE THIRTY TWO
REVISION CHAPTER FIVE PAGE THIRTY SEVEN

IF NOT - GO BACK AND RE-READ AND RE-LEARN UNTIL YOU CAN!

CHAPTER 6 - THREE CARD READINGS

You should now have an understanding of the numbers and suits, giving you the ability to decipher the meaning of any of the spot cards. Hopefully learning the suits and then the number meanings will allow you to put these ideas together so that you can *always* figure out the intrinsic properties of a card by putting its suit and number together, even if you don't know the meaning of an individual card the moment you see it.

We've already tried our hand at three card suit readings and managed to find quite a lot to say with very little information. With the numbers one to ten, coupled with the suit of each card in a three card reading we have a much greater amount of information to talk about.

Like the suit only readings, at the start of a standard three card reading you should get a quick overall feel for the reading as a whole by looking at the colours only.

Once you've decided on the overall shape of the reading using the colours, you should focus on deciphering the first card. Like I've said before, the first card isn't necessarily 'in the past' but may just be the first thing in the sequence that is going to happen. After you've decided what the first card means you treat that as the focus and see what influence the second card has on it.

Once you've done that, you treat the middle card as the focus, decipher that card and then decide what influence the third card has on the second one.

Finally when that is done you look over all the cards, see which suits and numbers are repeated and see if you can add anything else to the reading by adding up the card numbers.

THREE CARD READING:

1. *Lay three cards face up in a row*
2. *Figure out what the first card means*
3. *Figure out what the second card means and how it influences the first card*
4. *Figure out what the third card means and how it influences the second card*
5. *Take into account which suits and/or numbers appear more than once*
6. *See if any other interesting and relevant numbers can be created from adding up the first two cards, second two cards or all the cards to see if this can add some further insight into the reading*

The following thirteen examples were created entirely at random from a pack with the court cards removed. As such some of the readings are fairly easy to understand and decipher, and some are a bit confusing and open ended - just like they will be when you give your own readings. You need to accept that sometimes things aren't clear cut and you will often struggle to figure out what is going on! Don't worry - it's normal.

In these examples the colours are listed below each set of three cards, with a brief overview of what that colour reading could mean written in italics underneath the written names of the cards.

3♣ 6♦ 4♠
Black Red Black

THREE OF CLUBS / SIX OF DIAMONDS / FOUR OF SPADES
Things have taken a turn for the better, but it's not over yet

Taking a quick glance at the colours of the cards, we get the overall impression that things have been tough, they're going to get better but there's still some difficulties to be worked out in the future - the last card being a spade makes this even more apparent.

The reading starts with the Three of Clubs, which is all about ideas taking shape in and around work - the 'expansion' of the number Three with the influence of the Club - the work and socialising suit. With the Three of Clubs as the focus and the Six of Diamonds as the influence we have the positive and strong ideas of communication and money. It could be that things are looking up regarding these work ideas taking shape and if there hasn't been news about an injection of money as yet it could come soon. As the Six is about communication and the Diamonds are about money and power this is all quite a good influence on the Three of Clubs.

Moving on to the Six of Diamonds we can see that this is influenced by the Four of Spades. The four is home life related, and as a Spade this spells trouble at home influencing the communication and money aspect of the Six of Diamonds. Perhaps there's some problem with work creating friction at home, or it could be that the sources of the money are themselves being restricted by home life and other commitments. Whatever it is, it's obviously something that has to be sorted out before things can move on.

There's no heart in this set of three cards - it most definitely is a three card reading about work and home life colliding to some extent. None of the suits are doubled up - there's just one of each. The numbers are all quite low so these are things happening from the start to the middle of a cycle.

There's also no court cards so no people come directly into the reading - however as the Six is about communication then there are obviously people involved!

Other things to bear in mind:

The first two cards add up to nine, the number of 'things coming to fruition'. The last two cards add up to ten, the number of 'plans finalising'. All three cards add up to thirteen, which is widely regarded as an unlucky number. However, it also means the King in a pack of cards, the King being the thirteenth card counting the Jack and Queen as eleven and twelve respectively. So perhaps that could indicate a male influence in the background.

A♦ 2♠ 8♥   ACE OF DIAMONDS / TWO OF SPADES / EIGHT OF HEARTS
Red Black Red   *You're entering a rough patch but things will get better*

Taking a quick glance at the colours of the cards, we get the overall impression that things are pretty good but there's going to be a small rough patch either now or sooner rather than later.

The reading starts with the Ace of Diamonds, an extremely good card of fortune, fresh starts and monetary luck. With the Ace of Diamonds as the focus and the Two of Spades as the influence we have the disharmony of partnerships. The two is about coming together and of course the Spade is a the negative suit, so it looks like that for all the power of the Ace of Diamonds, there is a certain amount of disharmony going on somewhere which threatens to undermine things somewhat.

Moving on to the Two of Spades we can see that this is influenced by the Eight of Hearts. The eight is about getting out there and making things happen, and as a Heart this could well be about family or even romantic matters. As the Eight of Hearts is directly influencing a two then is could well be romantic issues coming to bear on a particular relationship. Let's not forget however that we have ended on a 'good' red card and it's a heart, so it may well be that these issues can be resolved.

There's no club in this three card reading - so it really is all about this relationship thing and the powerful Ace of Diamonds. What could it all mean? Perhaps there's a windfall which puts an excessive amount of strain on a relationship? Perhaps there's arguing over money, even though there's plenty of it it's become petty and annoying? Whatever it's about it does seem to get itself resolved, and this could be through family, friends or even a current lover. Or it could just be that the differences are resolved and everything is fine again after a tough patch.

There's no court cards in this reading, even though the two and the Hearts bring up these ideas of relationships and family.

Other things to bear in mind:

The first two cards add up to three, the number of expansion. This could indicate that things will move on and bring closer union. The last two cards add up to ten, the completion of plans. All three cards add up to eleven which is the number of the Jack in the pack. Could this indicate that there is a younger man involved? Now there's something to think about!

10♣ 6♣ 3♠ **TEN OF CLUBS / SIX OF CLUBS / THREE OF SPADES**
Black Black Black *The continuation of a tough spell*

Taking a quick glance at the colours of the cards, we get the overall impression of doom and gloom! However there is only one Spade in the reading at the end, so it can't be ALL bad. However getting an all black reading does signify that caution must be taken not to upset anyone or jumping to rash conclusions.

The reading starts with the Ten of Clubs, a very good card indeed dealing with the fruitful outcome of business and career related activities. Like all of the tens it's a fairly clear-cut card and it is always good to see at ten in a reading (apart from the Ten of Spades of course!) With the Ten of Clubs as the focus and the Six of Clubs as the influence, we have yet another work related card, this time to do with communication. Whatever is going on, big things are certainly going on in the workplace or in social and work related matters, and as there are two clubs side by side this can only really be seen as a positive and good thing. The Ten of Clubs is the best work related card so it's all good stuff.

Moving on to the Six of Clubs we can see that this is influenced by the Three of Spades. The three is about developments and expansion of ideas, but because it's a Spade this indicates there is some problem with that. The communicating business ideas of the Six of Clubs look like they're being held back by the Three of Spades. It could be that communications will get a bit messed up at the end of a project that was otherwise doing extremely well, or that somehow something gets lost in translation and things are unable to expand as planned.

There is no Diamond or Heart in this three card reading - this one most definitely is all about the work and not about the play!

Other things to bear in mind:

Although this is an all black card reading, there are two clubs in the reading and one of them is a ten, which is a very powerful card. The Three of Spades, although it is at the end of the reading is a fairly low card and it is somewhat overpowered by the two work related Clubs. It's important to always see which suits are the most dominant as this, like the overall colour shape, is an important factor in determining what forces have the most influence.

This also proves that the colour reading is a general guideline only and that every aspect of a reading must be taken into consideration before you deliver your verdict.

5♠ 2♥ 7♦ **FIVE OF SPADES / TWO OF HEARTS / SEVEN OF DIAMONDS** 4
Black Red Red *Entering and staying in a good phase*

Taking a quick glance at the colours of the cards, we get the overall impression that things are going to get better, not just in the future but quite soon if not immediately.

The reading starts with the Five of Spades, and we know that the number five is to do with growth. Unfortunately as it's a Spade this is to do with lack of growth and difficulties getting things moving. With the Five of Spades as the focus with the influence of the Two of Hearts, it looks like these problems could well be coming from a loved one. The two is for partnerships and as it's a Heart this is one of the most romantic cards in the pack - it looks like a very close loved one could well be part of the problem. However this reading is on the whole meant to be a positive one as we have two red cards, so it could be that this concept is flipped on its head and the difficulties could be overcome with the help of a loved one.

Moving on to the Two of Hearts itself we can see the the Seven of Diamonds is its influence. The Seven is to do with the spiritual and the Diamonds are for strength and power, so this Two of Hearts with it's ideas of love and partnerships also has the aspect of greater and higher things and could well be a more spiritual and deeper kind of love or relationship. It looks like the adversities presented by the Five of Spades really could be overcome with a lot of love from friends, family and with the aspect of the seven, a lover, or as Diamonds are of course to do with money, a financial windfall from an unexpected source.

There is no club in this three card reading so there is nothing in the cards that indicate work as such. It could be then that the struggle in question is more of an emotional block than 'real world' block. It could simply be a period of struggle for personal growth, helped along with those that can help.

Other things to bear in mind:

The first two cards add up to seven, again the spiritual number. And the last two cards add up to nine, another good number to do with things moving at a brisk pace for completion. It looks like that although we have a spade in the reading things could well turn out for the best.

7♣ 5♦ 10♥ SEVEN OF CLUBS / FIVE OF DIAMONDS / TEN OF HEARTS   5
Black Red Red *Entering and staying in a good phase*

Taking a quick glance at the colours of the cards, we get the overall impression that things are going to get better, not just in the future but quite soon if not immediately.

The reading starts with the Seven of Clubs, and the number seven is to do with higher things. As it's a Club this makes the whole card be about inventive and inspirational ideas at work and in the wider scheme of things. With the focus on this entrepreneurial and go-getting card and the influence of the Five of Diamonds this looks to be an incredibly good combination. The growth of plans already in motion of the five coupled with the power and money aspect of Diamonds means that these innovative and clever ideas are really going to get some real traction.

Moving on to the Five of Diamonds itself we can see the Ten of Hearts is the influence. As it's a ten this is a very powerful card of plans and ideas coming to fruition, and as a Heart these are most definitely romantic or family plans. The movement and development of the Five of Diamonds could well be driven by the Ten of Hearts. It could indicate a family team effort, or could also show the goodwill generated after the successful completion of a project. As we start with a Club one could assume that all of this is to do with work. However it could also be that work leads to some kind of romantic connection further down the line.

There is no Spade in this three card reading which indicates a fair amount of plain sailing.

Other things to bear in mind:

The first two cards add up to twelve, which indicates the Queen. With the idea of romance coming up in the reading, perhaps this could be a woman - a lover or a mother perhaps? All three cards add up to twenty two, which in numerology is seen as a very good number indeed.

A♥ 8♣ 2♣   ACE OF HEARTS / EIGHT OF CLUBS / TWO OF CLUBS
Red Black Black   *Entering and staying in a rough patch*

Taking a quick glance at the colours of the cards, we get the overall impression that things have been fine but are now entering a harder spell.

The reading starts with the Ace of Hearts, and right off the bat we have one of the strongest cards in the pack dealing with love and family. Aces are sometimes hard to understand on their own so we need to lean quite heavily on the next card to figure it out. With the focus on the Ace of Hearts and the influence of the Eight of Clubs we have the added idea of things moving rapidly in the workplace and socially. This is quite a powerful pairing - the power of love, charisma and goodwill with a very rapidly moving situation on the work and social front.

Moving on to the Eight of Clubs we can see that the Two of Clubs is the influence. Again we have another work related Club, and as it's a two this brings with it the idea of co-operation and partnerships at work and socially. The activity at work could be spurred on by working with others and forging alliances. And with there being a two, as well as starting the reading with the Ace of Hearts, this means there could well be love in the air at work! Although there isn't a Two of Hearts here, which usually signifies a lover or relationship, the idea of partnerships is fairly strong in this reading. It's not totally clear but there could well something romantic going on at work.

There is no Spade or Diamond in this reading, so there's nothing difficult going on, but without a Diamond there isn't any indication of financial gain or power. Perhaps we're looking at an increase in social standing as well in this reading, as opposed to earning more money. It could be that the whole reading is about going up in the world socially.

Other things to bear in mind:

The first two cards add up to nine, another great number of things moving at a rapid pace to a conclusion. The last two cards add up to ten giving us the idea of the actual conclusion itself! These are all great numbers so whatever happens it looks like it's going to be favourable.

Let's not forget we end with two black cards. Even though the cards in the reading are good, some caution is required. Perhaps things could get too heated - or dangerous, or even exciting. Watch out!

6♠ A♠ 3♦
Black Black Red

SIX OF SPADES / ACE OF SPADES / THREE OF DIAMONDS
Things have been tough but are going to get better in the future

Taking a quick glance at the colours of the cards, we get the overall impression that after a protracted spell of tough times, things are going to get better.

The reading starts with the Six of Spades, the six being about communication and with it being a Spade, a lack of communication. It could signify bad news. With the Six of Spades as the focus and the Ace of Spades as the influence it could be very bad news indeed. This is definitely going to be tough. It could be that the bad news has already come and the person you are reading for may know exactly what that is.

Moving on to the Ace of Spades itself we can see that the Three of Diamonds is its influence. The three being about growth coupled with the Diamond means this card is all about financial growth. However as this is influencing the difficult Ace of Spades it could be that in the future the difficulties arising from the first two Spades are counteracted to some extent by financial things working out better than expected - some money, or at least ideas involving money, could take off and soften the blow, whatever it may be.

There is no Heart in this reading and no Club, so these troubles don't seem to be about family or work. It could be about personal problems and life struggles that all get the better of us sometimes. It could be a problem of communication to the outside world, a feeling that one is detached from reality. Whatever it is, it seems the Three of Diamonds is there with a glimmer of hope financially to pull the person out of it.

Other things to bear in mind:

The first two cards add up to seven, the number of higher things. In some ways this could feed in to the idea of loss of nerve or a personal crisis. The last two cards add up to four, the number of stability. This helps the hope just a little bit.

Overall this is a tough reading to figure out, as it always is when you get two or three Spades in a reading. Sometimes things are just confusing for everybody!

9♥ 7♥ 9♠ NINE OF HEARTS / SEVEN OF HEARTS / NINE OF SPADES   8
Red Red Black *It's been plain sailing so far, but look out for clouds on the horizon*

Taking a quick glance at the colours of the cards, we get the overall impression that things are going pretty well into the near future but will take a turn for the worse a little bit later.

The reading starts with the Nine of Hearts, the Nine being about the rapid movement of things and coupled with Hearts these things are romantic or family orientated. The Nine of Hearts is a good card, of nice happy things moving along at a brisk pace. With the Nine of Hearts as the focus and another Heart, the seven, as the influence we also have the idea of a higher kind of love, of the deep and spiritual kind. In a way you could see the Seven of Hearts as being about faith as much as love.

Moving on to the Seven of Hearts we can see that the Nine of Spades is the influence. This is a tough Spade, as it's a nine it's about things moving rapidly to their conclusion and not obviously the ones that someone would like. So it appears that the spiritual Seven of Hearts is completely undermined by the Spade. Perhaps this is about a loss of faith? We have two nines in this reading, one being one of the best nines, the other being one of the worst. It could be that there's an ideological struggle going on here. The lofty ideals of the Nine of Hearts, the pain and worry of the Nine of Swords, and the Seven of Hearts in the middle, attempting to balance things out with its lofty ideals. It's almost as if there's some kind of conceit going on here.

This is quite a perplexing reading! It's certainly not simple and it seems quite contradictory. Whatever it is, it looks like there's going to be a lot of soul searching required - although it appears to have the potential to balance itself out. There's no Diamonds or Clubs, so there's nothing work related or financially rewarding about any of this - it all appears to be very emotional.

Other things to bear in mind:

When you get two numbers the same in a reading it's interesting to see how they work together. Here, they're one each side, sandwiching the Seven of Hearts in the middle. They're also such different nines it can only mean struggle and conflict between the two ideas. Caught in the middle is this idea of spirituality. It's overall quite a deep reading as there's nothing concrete or day to day living about it whatsoever - it's all head in the clouds stuff.

5♣ 4♦ 4♥ **FIVE OF CLUBS / FOUR OF DIAMONDS / FOUR OF HEARTS**
Black Red Red *Entering and staying in a good phase*

Taking a quick glance at the colours of the cards, we get the overall impression that things are going to get better, not just in the future but quite soon if not immediately.

The reading starts with the Five of Clubs, the five being about expansion and activity and the Clubs suit being about the workplace and social life. This is a solid 'things going well at work' card. With the Five of Clubs as the focus and the Four of Diamonds as the influence, we have the idea of solid finances - the four being about strong foundations and Diamonds being about money and power. So these two cards together are a very strong work and progression pairing meaning that as work continues at a good pace it is very much backed up by dependable sources.

Moving on the the Four of Diamonds we can see that the Four of Hearts is the influence. This is a four again, so the Four of Hearts indicates a strong dependable family influence on the Four Diamonds. With two fours in this reading there is certainly a lot of dependable energy going around. The idea of things moving well at work is backed up by the dependable Four of Diamonds with its money influence, and this is in turn backed up by the rock solid Four of Hearts with its influence of love, family and friends.

There's nothing particularly exciting or dramatic in this reading, but it is a good one nevertheless. There is no Spade in this reading and we have one of each of the other suits making this a well balanced and free from grief mix of cards.

Other things to bear in mind:

The first two cards add up to nine, a good number of things moving forward. The last two cards add up to eight, the number of getting out there and doing it. All three cards added together come to thirteen, the number of the King. It could be that there is some male influence in all of this.

5♥ 10♠ 6♥ FIVE OF HEARTS / TEN OF SPADES / SIX OF HEARTS   10
Red Black Red   *You're entering a rough patch but things will get better*

Taking a quick glance at the colours of the cards, we get the overall impression that things are pretty good but there's going to be a small rough patch either now or sooner rather than later.

The reading starts with the Five of Hearts, the five being about expansion and activity and the Hearts suit being about love and family life - this is a nice card to get regarding things moving along briskly on the home and love front. With the Five of Hearts as the focus and the Ten of Spades as the influence things are looking shaky indeed. The ten is the completion of a cycle, but being a Spade this is extremely ominous and could mean that some extremely challenging disruptions to home life are imminent.

Moving on to the Ten of Spades itself we can see that the Six of Hearts is the influence. The six is all about communication and being a Heart this is again about love and family. This could mean that the disquieting Ten of Spades is actually about getting news from and about one's family.

This is quite a hard set of cards to read. We have two Hearts either side of the Ten of Spades, which is widely regarded as the most challenging card in the pack. However, we do have two Hearts which together could just about overwhelm the 'badness' of the Ten of Spades. And also we do end on a red card, so the general outcome should be favourable. It does look like there are some extremely confusing and difficult times to come in the near future if not almost immediately, and although it appears that this is all about family problems, it is the strength of the family itself that makes things right.

There are no Clubs or Diamonds in this reading - it really is all about family and loved ones.

Other things to bear in mind:

It's easy to panic when you see the Ten of Spades. However you must remember that it's going to appear on average once in seventeen times (if you've giving three card readings that is). This is quite often! People don't have death and destruction in their lives anything like that much so you must treat these tough Spade cards as an indicator of challenges, obstacles and upheavals as opposed to fire and brimstone! Spades, although they indicate trouble and tough times, are fairly abstract without the other cards around them to give them meaning. And let us also remember that a warning is there to help prepare for the worst while we hope and aim for the best.

4♣ 9♦ 8♠ **FOUR OF CLUBS / NINE OF DIAMONDS / EIGHT OF SPADES** 11
Black Red Black *Things have taken a turn for the better, but it's not over yet*

Taking a quick glance at the colours of the cards, we get the overall impression that things have been tough, they're going to get better but there's still some difficulties to be worked out in the future - the last card being a spade makes this even more apparent.

The reading starts with the Four of Clubs, a good solid work card with the solid foundation of four coupled with the work and social aspect of Clubs. With the Four of Clubs as the focus and the Nine of Diamonds as the influence we have the power of the nine moving things to a good conclusion with the money and power of the Diamonds. Together these cards show a strong solid work and social aspect backed up by fast moving financial positives. Things are looking good for now.

Moving on to the Nine of Diamonds itself we can see that the Eight of Spades is the influence. Being a Spade this is a difficulty or hindrance, and being an eight which is about moving on with courage to pursue new ventures this indicates the opposite - a lack of courage and belief. With this influencing the exciting and powerful ideas held within the Nine of Diamonds it could be that although things are going incredibly well, a lack of nerve could undermine the whole thing.

Again it's hard to pinpoint exactly what the problem is as we only have a single Spade to go on, but as is usual it is likely to be a personal inner struggle as there is no other card to lean on to fully understand this difficulty. It does seem however that this is a case of defeat pulled from the jaws of victory, and with the Nine of Diamonds showing that things are so close to completion we can only assume that whoever this reading is for they must hold their nerve and not let over-thinking and worry get the better of them.

There is no Heart in this reading so this is most definitely a reading all about work, real life and the drama of what could be a high pressure situation!

Other things to bear in mind:

You're going to have to get used to extremely good cards being overshadowed by the Spades suit. Don't forget you have a one in four chance of picking one just by pulling a card from the pack. They are common cards! Sometimes the good cards are worth fighting for and you should always remember that Spades are not just about struggle but about fighting, being prepared and often winning. Just because there is an obstacle or a battle ahead doesn't mean it's insurmountable. The power of the Nine of Diamonds, always a good card to see, may be something the person having this reading may really have to fight for both externally in the real world and internally, with their nerves and resolve.

10♦ 9♣ A♣ **TEN OF DIAMONDS / NINE OF CLUBS / ACE OF CLUBS**
Red Black Black *Entering and staying in a rough phase*

Taking a quick glance at the colours of the cards, we get the overall impression that things have been fine but are now entering a harder spell.

The reading starts with the Ten of Diamonds, one of the best cards in the pack, the ten signifying the successful completion of a project or cycle and the suit of Diamonds showing that this has powerful implications and monetary gain. With the Ten of Diamonds as the focus and the Nine of Clubs as the influence we have another extremely good card, the Nine being about rushing to a successful conclusion and the suit of Clubs being about work - so the success and money of the Ten of Diamonds is most definitely about a project at work moving quickly and positively to completion with exciting and well earned success.

Moving on to the Nine of Clubs itself we can see that the Ace of Clubs is the influence - an extremely good card to see, again dealing with a work and social aspect, but unlike the Nine of Clubs, the Ace is about fresh starts, new beginnings and also the power of work and real life in general. This not only amplifies the Nine of Clubs and the Ten of Diamonds and makes things look even more rosy, but it shows that it could well be a case of out of the frying pan, into the fire - no sooner has the success at work with one thing finished, a brand new opportunity may arise taking things to even greater heights.

We must exercise caution however as the last two cards of this reading are black indicating that things could still go pear shaped. With this amount of goodwill and cheer and success in the cards, care must be taken for it not all go too far and to lose sight of what's important. This reading is so positive in many ways, it may be only the colours of the cards that serve as a warning to not be burned by the flames of success.

There are no Spades or Hearts in this reading, so seems to be no personal struggle in all of this and it is entirely in the domain of work and social life.

Other things to bear in mind:

The last two cards add up to ten giving us yet another ten for completion in the mix. Altogether the cards add up to twenty - two tens of course. It seems like there are lots of ends of cycles here, and although this is for the good, there is just this underlying feeling that sometimes when things really go your way in life, you can change and sometimes lose a little of something else.

8♦ 7♠ 3♥   EIGHT OF DIAMONDS / SEVEN OF SPADES / THREE OF HEARTS
Red Black Red   *You're entering a rough patch but things will get better*

Taking a quick glance at the colours of the cards, we get the overall impression that things are pretty good but there's going to be a small rough patch either now or sooner rather than later.

The reading starts with the Eight of Diamonds, the eight signifying making things move forward and with the Diamonds this is a card about having things happen successfully with your own hard work. With the focus on the Eight of Diamonds and the influence of the Seven of Spades we have the idea of higher things in the seven, and with being a Spade this could be seen as a loss of belief or spiritual crisis. The great ideas of the Eight of Diamonds may be being held back by worries and concerns that one makes up, even if they may not be at all real - a personal loss of faith perhaps.

With the Seven of Spades as the focus and the Three of Hearts as the influence we have the idea of the fruitful expansion of love and family. Perhaps it is this influence which can tame the worry of the Seven of Spades, or perhaps it's part of the problem? As this reading ends with a red card I would think it was the former - the difficulties experienced are overcome with the extension of love and family developments.

There are no Clubs in this reading, and one each of the other suits. So this is mainly about personal development, worry and the idea of family being there in times of trouble. It's interesting that we have the Three of Hearts as the calming influence however, seeing as that is about the expansion of love and making something from nothing.

Other things to bear in mind:

If you add the last two cards up they come to ten, the number of completion. That's a good sign, and perhaps means that these issues will be resolved better than expected.

Hopefully these examples show that giving a reading brings up as many questions as it attempts to answer. What work project? What kind of relationship? Money from where? It can all be quite baffling, especially when a reading can hold together well and make sense taken as a mere story, but the person you are giving the reading for cannot relate to it at all! You will also find that giving a reading for yourself can sometimes make no sense at all and appear completely irrelevant.

It happens. Some readings seem to make sense the moment you see the cards. At other times the cards appear completely disparate, disconnected and a complete chore to figure out. Don't take it personally.

Later on in the book I'll give you some other things you can do to make things a bit easier when the cards aren't giving much away. But first let's move on to the court cards so we can learn to fit them into a three card reading and finally be able to read with the whole pack.

PRACTICING GIVING THREE CARD READINGS

You have your working deck and your normal deck. You can now practice giving three card readings with your working deck until you feel comfortable with the meanings of the spot cards, and once you're somewhat confident you can test yourself with your normal deck.

Switching between your working deck and your normal deck will help you realise which cards you're having problems with. However your normal deck will eventually give you more of a sense of freedom as you will not have the words in front of you.

At first you may struggle to create three card readings with your normal deck, but by switching back and forth you should come to quite enjoy being able to decipher and read the normal cards without needing the words as a crutch.

As always, single out cards you're having particular problems with and give some practice readings using ONLY your problem cards.

REVISION: CHAPTER SIX

There's no point in asking revision questions at this stage - you have a deck of forty spot cards which you could potentially give practice readings with that are just waiting to be revised! Mix them up and practice giving three card readings until you feel pretty good about most of the cards.

Each card has the potential to have one of fifty one different cards to be placed after it as its 'influence'. That alone creates over two and a half thousand combinations if you include every card in the deck! You can't learn every combination by wrote, but hopefully you have enough information to piece things together by now. Add to that the third card of a three card reading and the possibilities are vast.

So the question is, can you shuffle the forty spot cards and do a three card practice reading and feel comfortable with unravelling the clues and signs in MOST readings? It's not about knowing every combination - it's about having enough knowledge and tools to understand pretty much ANY layout of cards. So to revise - just keep practising!

CHAPTER 7 - THE COURT CARDS

As mentioned earlier in this book, the court cards represent people. The Kings represents adult males, the Queens represent adult females and the Jacks represent youths who can be male or female. It is widely acknowledged that the red cards indicate a person of a fairer outward complexion than the black cards, with diamonds being 'the fairest' and spades being 'the darkest'. This shouldn't be taken too literally however.

As we now have a good understanding of the four suits it is fairly easy to imagine what type of person each court card represents. The Diamond court cards are powerful, rich and influential. The Club court cards are people in and around work and social life. The Heart court cards are family and lovers and the Spade court cards are people who would hinder rather than help us.

It's easy to think of these people as immediate family and friends (Hearts), your work colleagues and other acquaintances (Clubs), wealthier and more influential contacts (Diamonds) and people who aren't necessarily enemies but competitors (Spades).

As we have learned giving two and three card readings with just the spot cards, the order of the cards in a reading is important, each card shedding light on the previous card. Just like the spot cards, to truly understand the motives of a person represented by a court card we have to look at the influence of the other cards around them.

The Kings and Queens are the men and women of the world. These could be your father, your mother, your bank manager, your boss and all kinds of male and female influences. Men and women work in extremely different ways and fulfil very different roles in society depending on where you are in the world. A father figure is very different from a mother figure - and men have traditionally fought the battles while women have tended to their families. This is not to say both aren't powerful - but as we all know, men and women have different kinds of strength. Be wary of stereotypes in this transgender age.

The Jacks are the youths of the world. They may not have figured out who they are yet, but they bring energy, enthusiasm and sometimes confusion. The Jacks have another meaning as they are related to Knaves - messengers on horseback - so they can also mean the arrival of news and information. This in turn brings thoughts of the speed of youth, quick-wittedness and things moving at a brisk pace.

As a rough guide the red Jacks represent young women and girls and the black Jacks represent young men and boys. Once again this way of figuring out which Jacks are male and which are female isn't cast in stone - there is always room in the world for a boyish romantic like the Jack Of Hearts and an unruly teenager such as the Jack Of Spades could also be female.

In the following section we're going to take a look at each court card family. Alongside each card name in italicised print there are some suggestions as to what kind of role in society each person represented could play. These are merely suggestions and should not be taken literally - they are there to help you think along the right lines. For instance, the Queen of Diamonds could simply be a woman in your life who influences you financially such as an aunt who has lent you money!

Figuring out who these people are in a reading is hugely dependant on the person you are reading for - they are the ones who will 'recognise' the court cards with your help. You can only really assist them in this by giving them some background on each court card and taking the surrounding cards into account.

THE COURT DIAMONDS

The court diamonds represent powerful, wealthy and influential individuals

K♦   **KING OF DIAMONDS**   *Bank manager, professor, financial angel*

               A powerful man. A wealthy man. An influential man.
               Clever, quick witted and well read.

Q♦   **QUEEN OF DIAMONDS**   *Bank manager, professor, financial angel*

               A powerful woman. A wealthy woman. An influential woman.
               Clever, quick witted and well read.

J♦   **JACK OF DIAMONDS**   *A student, a young risk taker / entrepreneur*

               A powerful youth. A wealthy youth. An influential youth.
               A privileged youth born into money and influence.

               The Jack brings news: Money related news

THE COURT CLUBS

The court clubs represent people from one's workplace and social life

K♣   **KING OF CLUBS**   *Your boss, a superior, a major work influence*

               A man in the workplace. A man you know socially.
               Practical, down to earth, progressive. Entrepreneurial.

Q♣   **QUEEN OF CLUBS**   *Your boss, a superior, a major work influence*

               A woman in the workplace. A woman you know socially.
               Practical, down to earth, progressive. Entrepreneurial.

J♣   **JACK OF CLUBS**   *An apprentice, a youthful part-timer, a volunteer*

               A youth in the workplace. A youth you know socially. Entrepreneurial.
               A driven career-minded youth with potential and energy.

               The Jack brings news: Work related news

THE COURT HEARTS

The court hearts are family members, friends and lovers

K♥ **KING OF HEARTS** *Husband / father / lover / close male friend*

    An important male family member, friend, lover or fan
    Emotional, empathic and friendly

Q♥ **QUEEN OF HEARTS** *Wife / mother / lover / close female friend*

    An important female family member, friend, lover or fan
    Emotional, empathic and friendly

J♥ **JACK OF HEARTS** *Son / daughter / young friend or lover*

    An important younger family member, friend, lover or fan
    Emotional, empathic and friendly

    The Jack brings news: A compliment, a gift, a date

THE COURT SPADES

The court spades are those who would oppose us or get in our way

K♠ **KING OF SPADES** *Male police officer / man in uniform / judge*

    A formidable male opponent to one's plans
    A male authority figure, a man with a grudge, a loner, a depressive

Q♠ **QUEEN OF SPADES** *Female police officer / female in uniform / judge*

    A formidable female opponent to one's plans
    An female authority figure, a woman with a grudge, a loner, a depressive

J♠ **JACK OF SPADES** *An unruly teenager / a spiteful youngster*

    A youthful yet formidable opponent to one's plans
    An untrustworthy youth, confused, edgy, bitter and detached

    The Jack brings news: Bad news in general

Hopefully by now, with your knowledge of the suits and having gone through the spot cards, applying the suits to the court cards makes relative sense. Unlike the spot cards which can be rather abstract, the court cards are actually about people so are easier to get to grips with.

Saying that, it should be noted that the court cards don't ALWAYS denote people. They can represent raw human power in the world of people. For instance, the King Of Clubs could represent an entire company, the Queen Of Spades could represent an institution, and as we've already discussed, the Jacks can mean a message.

So when is a court card not a person and simply a 'force of nature'? Simply put, if any particular court card isn't immediately apparent as a person in someone's life, one should attempt to look at the court card in this new way. When there is doubt, we need to lean on the other cards in the reading to figure out what this card signifies.

We must remember though that a court card that is not recognised may simply be someone that the person having the reading hasn't met yet. Where the court cards fall in a reading can make a lot of difference - people we have yet to meet are most definitely in our future!

So far we've looked at how the suits influence each other, how these influence the numbers one to ten, and how these individual cards work together in a reading, but we've yet to see what happens when we throw the court cards into the mix. Before we look at some examples we're going to have to finish making up our working pack.

Action: The only cards you have yet to write on in your working pack are the court cards. There is far less white space on the court cards so we're going to take it for granted that you understand what the suits mean and what age of person each card represents. Simply write four aspects of each court card on the sides of each card. Don't write the specifics (bank manager, husband etc) - just the concepts.

There now follows ten examples of three card readings using the whole deck with the court cards included. Each example has at least one court card so you can see what happens when the people in our lives show up in a reading. These cards were again picked at random from a normal deck - no point being unrealistic!

5♠ 4♥ J♦ **FIVE OF SPADES / FOUR OF HEARTS / JACK OF DIAMONDS**
Black Red Red *Entering and staying in a good phase*

Taking a quick glance at the colours of the cards, we get the overall impression that things are going to get better, not just in the future but quite soon if not immediately.

The reading starts with the Five of Spades, the five signifying growth at home and in things that are already formed, but as it's a Spade this is a problem with development and could mean there's some kind of stagnation going on. With the focus on the Five of Spades and the influence of the Four of Hearts, we have the stability of the four with love and warmth of the Heart coming to bear on this problem. This is not a bad thing - it looks like whatever is getting stuck somewhere is going to be helped with loved ones at home.

With the focus on the Four of Hearts and with the influence of the Jack of Diamonds we know that there is a young person involved who is responsible for this stability and help. This could be an outside influence or could be a member of the family. If it's an outside influence then their help could be monetary, and if it's family then their powerful influence could be of the helping and healing kind.

The Jack could also be news, possibly involving a young person, that is part of this helping and stabilising Four of Hearts. It could be that news will come from someone that is expected but has yet to be known, and it is this that alleviates the symptoms of the Five of Spades.

There are no Clubs in this reading, so it's definitely nothing to do with work problems. It all appears to be a bit of a problem with home life that works out well in the end.

Other things to bear in mind:

The first two card add up to nine, the number of things speeding up to completion. This adds to the idea that things will be resolved successfully.

As this is the first example reading in this section, it's worth noting what happens when you add the court cards into a reading - there is a trade-off of information. We gain a person, who may or may not be someone we or whoever we're reading for know, but the court cards don't shine as much conceptual light as the spot cards. A person is a person and that's that, and even though in this case the Jack could also be seen as 'news' there is something fairly definite about having any court card show up in a reading. You find that you have to lean on the remaining cards more to figure out what the whole reading is all about.

Q♥ 2♥ 7♥ QUEEN OF HEARTS / TWO OF HEARTS / SEVEN OF HEARTS
Red Red Red *The continuation of a good phase*

Taking a quick glance at the colours of the cards, we can see that everything is looking good in the past, present and future with no problems or obstacles in the way.

We start with the Queen of Hearts, so this reading begins with a definite person that we know could be your or someone's partner, mother or other important female figure. If you're a man, this is most definitely your wife, girlfriend or lover - or perhaps a woman who has yet to come in to your life. If you're a woman it could be you! With the focus on the Queen of Hearts and the influence of the Two of Hearts we have the partnership number of two coupled with the most romantic suit in the deck - another Heart. The Two of Hearts is pretty much always about good relationships and fruitful partnerships so it's fairly apparent that this Queen of Hearts, whoever she represents, is going to be getting a lot closer - if that's possible!

With the focus on the Two of Hearts and the influence of the Seven of Hearts we have the idea of higher more spiritual things with the seven and with it AGAIN being a Heart this is a card of a higher love, fulfilment and joy. The Two of Hearts can't have really got much better, but with this influence it's incredibly powerful.

It would be almost impossible if you were a man having this reading to not see the whole thing as some kind of deeply romantic metaphor. Either you're going to meet the woman of your dreams, or the love you already have with a woman is going to get ever deeper and more fulfilling. If you're a woman then the Queen of Hearts could be you, learning to love yourself and experience almost spiritual love and fulfilment!

There's no other card but Hearts in this reading. Love conquers all! I get a smile on my face just looking at these cards - you don't get much better than that.

Other things to bear in mind:

It's pretty rare to get overwhelmingly positive readings like this. You might find that the whole thing just seems completely irrelevant to someone who is miserable and whose life has run aground. The only thing it can mean in those circumstances is great change.

Similarly if you have a reading where all the cards are Spades and the whole thing is complete doom and gloom it can be hard to know what to make of it, especially if you're dealing with someone who is full of beans and whose life is going great. It could imply that their happiness is about to be challenged and that they may come to have trouble keeping their happiness going. Spades alone very rarely tell us much however - I tend to draw extra cards and I'll come to that idea later!

5♦ 7♠ K♥ **FIVE OF DIAMONDS / SEVEN OF SPADES / KING OF HEARTS**   3
Red Black Red
You're entering a rough patch but things will get better

Taking a quick glance at the colours of the cards, we get the overall impression that things are pretty good but there's going to be a small rough patch either now or sooner rather than later.

We start with the Five of Diamonds, so we begin with the five meaning growth from stable underpinnings with the Diamond of monetary gain. With the Five of Diamonds as the focus and the Seven of Spades as the influence however we have the idea of higher thought becoming confused - the Seven of Spades is about losing faith in oneself as as in higher things. So whatever good things that are coming from the Five of Diamonds this is being undermined by the rather downtrodden thinking of the Seven of Spades.

With the Seven of Spades as the focus and the King of Hearts as the influence we can see that all this negativity could well be helped from an adult family member such as a father, or even a male partner. The reading ends in a red card so we know that everything will be fine, so this male figure looks like they're going to be a great help while the person having the reading sorts out their personal problems so they can move on.

There's no Clubs in this reading so there's nothing work related here.

Other things to bear in mind:

When I first analysed this reading I'd forgotten to take into account that the reading ended in a red card and had the King of Hearts cast as some kind of villain who was responsible for the heartache of the Seven of Spades! It just shows you should be careful before you jump to conclusions and always take the colours, the shape and all the suits into consideration before you start creating monsters out of people's family and friends!

8♥ J♦ 10♠ EIGHT OF HEARTS / JACK OF DIAMONDS / TEN OF SPADES
Red Red Black *It's been plain sailing so far, but look out for clouds on the horizon*

Taking a quick glance at the colours of the cards, we get the overall impression that things are going pretty well into the near future but will take a turn for the worse a little bit later.

We start with the Eight of Hearts, so we begin with the eight which is all about having the strength of character to go out and do things coupled with Hearts, meaning this is a card all about self belief in your looks and romantic affairs. With the focus on the Eight of Hearts and the influence of the Jack of Diamonds, we have the idea of a young wealthy or powerful person coming to bear on this strength. Perhaps this Jack of Diamonds person is enabling and strengthening the Eight of Hearts, maybe with a romantic twist?

With the Jack of Diamonds as the focus and the Ten of Spades as the influence we have this most difficult card muddying the water. Now it could be that the fortunes of this youthful and enterprising young person are short lived, however good his or her intensions - or it could be that this person is in fact crooked to the bone! It is rather hard to tell so the best thing to say here is to show some caution. The Ten of Spades could also mean that this youthful influence could simply be unstable, no matter how much goodwill he or she brings.

There's no Clubs in this reading so there's nothing work related here.

Other things to bear in mind:

The eight and the ten are both at the end of the cycle of ten. It could indicate that this particular phase is coming to an end.

This reading brought up the idea of a card actually affecting someone else, in this case whoever is represented by the Jack of Diamonds. As you can see, we have to judge and discuss whether a spot card after a court card is telling us more about the person's character, or is telling us about things that could happen to them at some point. Let's not forget that whatever happens here, the person shown is represented by a 'good' card - it would be a different matter if we were talking about the Jack of Spades for instance. Whatever the Ten of Spades represents, it would seem that it's out of the Jack's hands.

Let's not forget about that internal and external struggle of Spades that I've talked about in previous sections. Perhaps this Jack of Diamonds has his own deep personal problems which are difficult for even him to fathom out? It doesn't make him any less powerful, but who knows?

9♦ 3♥ Q♣   **NINE OF DIAMONDS / THREE OF HEARTS / QUEEN OF CLUBS**
Red Red Black   *It's been plain sailing so far, but look out for clouds on the horizon*

Taking a quick glance at the colours of the cards, we get the overall impression that things are going pretty well into the near future but will take a turn for the worse a little bit later.

We start with the Nine of Diamonds, a card all about being on the cusp of powerful and financial rewards. With the focus on the Nine of Diamonds and the influence of the Three of Hearts we have the idea of love and expansion in the family and at home. These two cards really appear strong together and it's almost as if a marriage or children are going to lead to a more fulfilled life. It's hard to see where money fits in with all this really, although the expansion of family life could of course involve selling a property to move in to a better and bigger one!

With the Three of Hearts as the focus and the Queen of Clubs as the influence, we have the idea of a strong female work colleague or socialite coming to bear on this love and family stuff. This isn't necessarily a bad thing, but we do end on a black card so this could be someone at work putting pressure on home and family life for the worse. To follow through with the previous idea, a female co-worker or boss not being happy with a family move for instance.

However there are no 'bad' cards in this reading so it's hard to be all doom and gloom about it. But this lady will be playing a part in future events according to this reading.

There's no Spades in this reading so like I said there's nothing really that difficult going on!

Other things to bear in mind:

The nine and the three both add up to twelve, which is again the number of the Queen. Perhaps she pervades this situation even more as her influence is felt even in the first two cards alone!

As I said before, as there's no Spades there's nothing untoward going on as there are no Spades, so the Queen could be influential but not in any sinister way.

K♣ Q♦ 10♣
Black Red Black

KING OF CLUBS / QUEEN OF DIAMONDS / TEN OF CLUBS
Things have taken a turn for the better, but it's not over yet

Taking a quick glance at the colours of the cards, we get the overall impression that things have been tough, they're going to get better but there's still some difficulties to be worked out in the future.

We start with the King of Clubs, a male character related to work, business and social standing. As we are at the beginning of the reading it is most likely to be someone that we know as they are in our present! When you start with a court card in a reading it is pretty tough to assess who this person is - if you're giving yourself a reading it may be pretty obvious, but if you are reading for someone else this could take a while to fathom out.

With the King of Clubs as the focus and the influence of the Queen of Diamonds we have here an influential and perhaps wealthy woman influencing this King! We've started the reading with two court cards so whoever these people are they must be important. Perhaps one of these court cards actually represents us, or the person we are reading for? It's hard to tell - yet some people will immediately point to a card once you've explained who it could be and will say 'oh yes that's me'.

So, if you or the person you are reading for identifies with one of these court cards you must treat it as 'them' for the rest of the reading. Of course, this could happen during ANY reading where there is a court card involved. My advice is, don't disagree. If someone really clicks with a court card or thinks it's them, go with it. They're probably right.

So far this reading has been a bit of a mystery and we have two characters, either of which may be relevant, or both, or neither! Perhaps the King of Clubs isn't actually a person, but represents 'work' or a corporation. Or perhaps the King is YOU and the Queen is influencing YOU in some way?

This of course shows up the limits of practicing giving readings just to yourself or learning from a book. You can only start working with this kind of thing on the job - by actually giving readings. More on that later!

So the Ten of Clubs, a terrific work completion card, is influencing this woman, the Queen of Diamonds. She's coming to the end of a work cycle and all is good there. We have two Clubs in this reading so it is heavily work dominated, so in a nutshell there are big things going on at work, and this powerful lady is right in the thick of it. However she's not a Club - she is a different kind of power of influence and potentially money.

I'll be honest, this reading is very difficult to describe in a book. If you were to give this reading to and with another human being you could both piece it together and have a lot of fun doing so!

9♠ J♠ 2♦ NINE OF SPADES / JACK OF SPADES / TWO OF DIAMONDS
Black Black Red *Things have been tough but are going to get better in the future*

Taking a quick glance at the colours of the cards, we get the overall impression that after a protracted spell of tough times, things are going to get better.

We start with the Nine of Spades, a not terribly good card dealing with missed opportunities and 'clutching defeat from the jaws of victory' as I sometimes call it. With the focus on the Nine of Spades and the influence of the Jack of Spades we have a young person who's a bit of a sly one and can't really be trusted. So whatever is going to go a bit pear-shaped is possibly because of this Jack of Spades character.

With the focus on the Jack of Spades and the influence of the Two of Diamonds we have the notion of a partnership involving money or power. It could be that this youth is involved in a partnership with either you or whoever you're giving the reading for, and there's money involved.

We've ended on an upbeat note with the red Two of Diamonds, so whatever happens and no matter how cheated one may feel at the hands of this person either directly or indirectly, something good will come out of it. It could be that the financial partnership of the Two of Diamonds is nothing to do with the Jack and it is this that finally thwarts his manoeuvres.

This is one of those readings where it would be really interesting to draw another card for some extra clarification. More on that later.

There are no Clubs in this reading so it's most definitely nothing to do with work.

Other things to bear in mind:

The nine and the two add up to eleven - also the number of the Jack. This would appear to give the Jack even more gravitas than it has already! It's all about the Jack in this reading.

There's also two Spades in this reading - not great it has to be said!

Let's also not forget that the Jack of Spades could signify bad news - how do you think that would affect the reading?

J♣ A♦ Q♠   JACK OF CLUBS / ACE OF DIAMONDS / QUEEN OF SPADES
Black Red Black   *Things have taken a turn for the better, but it's not over yet*

Taking a quick glance at the colours of the cards, we get the overall impression that things have been tough, they're going to get better but there's still some difficulties to be worked out in the future - the last card being a spade makes this even more apparent.

We start with the Jack of Clubs - a young person who could be a work colleague or someone known socially. With the focus on the Jack of Clubs and the influence of the Ace of Diamonds we have the pure force of power, influence and money coming into play. Whatever this Jack of Clubs is doing he or she has or is about to get a massive boost either financially or diplomatically. The Jack either brings this power already to the table, or is about to receive it - perhaps unknowingly. It's hard to tell!

With the focus on the Ace of Diamonds and the influence of the Queen of Spades we have a female adult coming into play who would seem to be able to mess this all up. Notice this Queen doesn't directly influence the Jack, but the power of the Ace of Diamonds - she's able to directly affect this raw power somehow. Whatever she's up to, she's likely to put a spanner in the works and is certainly going to be putting obstacles in the way of the Jack of Clubs.

There are no Hearts in this reading, so there's nothing romantic going on here! More of a power struggle.

Other things to bear in mind:

There is only one spot card, the Ace of Diamonds, in the reading flanked by two court cards. As we have discussed and learnt, the Aces are a lot to do with the raw power of each suit. They are also about new starts, so this Jack could be something to do with a new venture involving money or social mobility that this Queen of Spades is getting in the way of. The reading ends on a black card and has two black cards in it, and usually I would say that things may end up rather sour. However, the Aces are powerful cards, and with some judgement I would say that all is not lost and the power and muscle of this Ace of Diamonds can still shine, if we can learn how to deal with this destructive Queen!

We could really do with some more info on these cards...

Let's also not forget that the Jack of Clubs could refer to some work related news - how would that affect the reading?

9♣ K♠ 4♦   **NINE OF CLUBS / KING OF SPADES / FOUR OF DIAMONDS**
Black Black Red   *Things have been tough but are going to get better in the future*

Taking a quick glance at the colours of the cards, we get the overall impression that after a protracted spell of tough times, things are going to get better.

We start with the Nine of Clubs, a card all about work and projects nearing completion. With the focus on the Nine of Clubs and with the influence of the King of Spades we have a man getting in the way and making things difficult. He could be part of the problem or could be an outside influence, it's hard to tell.

With the focus on the King of Spades and the influence of the Four of Diamonds we have the idea of solid and powerful foundations being laid for success and possible financial reward. We end with a red card, so looking on the bright side it appears that the King will be thwarted in his attempts to mess things up for the Nine by the strength of strong finances and stable affairs. If you keep your house in order, you can tolerate even the nastiest big bad wolf!

There are no Hearts in this reading so it's certainly not about love and families.

Other things to bear in mind:

This is quite a nice reading to talk about. It creates a simple story with some cards that seem to make sense together without trying too hard. As I said before, sometimes you get readings that come together really easily, and at other times you struggle to make things coherent.

However, talking about these cards without relating them to yourself or someone else (as we are having to do in this book) means we can get a bit smug about our ability to give readings. Don't forget that just because you can make a good story out of a reading, doesn't mean that the person you are giving the reading to won't derail the story that initially comes to your mind.

This point does illustrate just how much like a story readings can be. The cards let you tell a tale, and with interjections and suggestions from a third party (the person you are giving a reading for) you both create a semi-relevant narrative for this person.

Stories are powerful, and practicing telling stories with the cards is a great way to practice giving readings whilst at the same time becoming more familiar with the cards and the way they interact with each other.

3♦ K♦ 6♥ **THREE OF DIAMONDS / KING OF DIAMONDS / SIX OF HEARTS** 10
Red Red Red *The continuation of a good phase*

Taking a quick glance at the colours of the cards, we can see that everything is looking good in the past, present and future with no problems or obstacles in the way.

We start with the Three of Diamonds, a card all about the power and financial reward of developing ideas into a real form. If you were to imagine that the Three of Clubs was a good card for early business expansion and development, then the Three of Diamonds could be seen as your bank manager helping you out!

With the focus on the Three of Diamonds with the influence of the King of Diamonds we have a male character who is powerful and influential coming into the picture. As he's another Diamond this is extremely good news! The Three is getting help from this King and it's hard to think they wouldn't be intrinsically linked somehow. Things are moving forward with the help of this powerful man.

With the focus on the King of Diamonds and the influence of the Six of Hearts we have the idea of communication, families and love. Perhaps this King is a long lost relative who you hear is coming to help you out. The Six could be telling us that the King has romantic aspirations towards you and you will soon find out! Or perhaps it's the love of this King person that ultimately inspires the power and reward of the Three of Diamonds?

There are only red cards in this reading so everything is rosy. It's easy to see Diamonds and think of work connected with power and money, but there are no Clubs here so I would be wary to think that any of it was connected with work, even though it of course could be.

There are no Spades so there's certainly nothing bad here!

Other things to bear in mind:

Must admit I'm a bit stumped as to what the Six of Hearts is all about. It's influencing the powerful man in some way, but it's a bit vague. Perhaps he gets some information from his own family which helps him out, or some news.

Hmmm...

PRACTICING TELLING STORIES

As mentioned in the last few examples, giving a reading is somewhat like telling a story - as you decipher the cards of a reading the story unfolds but unlike a normal story you are using the cards as inspiration and seeing where it takes you.

However, when you are giving a reading to someone else you also have their own input as they listen to what you say about the cards, and explain which cards resonate with them the most. Although you can go so far with your own one-sided story, the art of giving a reading is in the interaction you have with whoever you're giving the reading for. They should not be just a listener but an active participant in the reading.

Don't forget it is THEY who will be pointing at the Queen of Diamonds saying 'Oh yes that's my aunt Doris' and not you. THEY will fill in the blanks. Allow them the space to join in and help you with your readings. Don't forget, they're the ones with the answers!

Action: Shuffle up your entire working deck and pull out a court card. Use this 'character' as the protagonist of a story you are about to create. Turning over one card at a time from the deck create a story about this initial person using the meanings of each card as you turn them over one at a time. Explain what happens to him and describe the people he meets, for good or for bad. Go through the whole pack if you can and try to keep the story cohesive! If you can do it with your working deck, then try it with your normal deck. This is great practice!

CHAPTER SEVEN REVIEW

THE COURT CARDS REPRESENT PEOPLE IN OUR LIVES

THE KINGS ARE MEN, THE QUEENS ARE WOMEN, AND THE JACKS ARE YOUNGER MEN, WOMEN, TEENS AND CHILDREN

WE NEED TO LEAN HEAVILY ON OTHER CARDS TO ASCERTAIN WHAT THE COURT CARDS MEAN

AS WE GIVE READINGS, WE NEED TO DISCOVER WHO THE PEOPLE UNCOVERED IN THE COURT CARDS ACTUALLY ARE - DO WE KNOW THEM OR ARE WE YET TO MEET THEM?

THE JACKS CAN ALSO MEAN NEWS AS THEY ALSO SIGNIFY KNIGHTS ON HORSEBACK

THE SPADE COURT CARDS ARE PEOPLE WHO WOULD GET IN OUR WAY, SPOIL OUR PLANS AND SOUR THE MOOD

REVISION: CHAPTER SEVEN

1. Are the Jacks considered male or female?

2. What types of people are the Queens and Kings?

3. Getting specific, what kind of person is the Jack of Hearts?

4. What's the difference between the Jack of Hearts and the Jack of Spades?

5. If the Queen of Clubs and the Queen of Hearts appeared in the same reading, what could that mean?

6. What types of 'real' people could the King of Diamonds represent?

7. One of the court cards could quite easily represent someone boss. Which one?

8. The Jack of Clubs is quite a specific character. What's he/she like?

9. There's a romantic woman on the horizon. Which card is she?

10. Who could the Queen of Diamonds be in your own life?

11. Who could the King of Hearts be in your own life?

12. The Jack of Spades meets the Queen of Diamonds. Explain how they get on.

13. The King of Hearts meets the Queen of Clubs. Describe their conversation.

14. The Jack of Hearts meets the King of Clubs and starts arguing about something. Can you describe what the conversation could/might go like?

15. Which court card is most likely to be your bank manager?

16. Which court card is most likely to be a police officer?

17. If you had to pick a card out that described YOU, which one would it be?

18. Think about three close friends and pick out a court card that you think describes each one of them the closest.

19. What other meaning do the Jacks have?

20. Who is the person most likely to know who the court cards in your readings represent?

CHAPTER 8 - DECK PERSONALITY

If you've read through all the examples so far, you'll have noticed that in writing this book I've become personally frustrated trying to describe the meanings of some of the readings, especially in the last section when the court cards were added and 'real' people and not just concepts were thrown into the mix.

The fact is that no matter how much I describe how each reading may be interpreted, and no matter how much I go on about how 'this card influences that card' I am missing the biggest influence of all - the person who is actually having the reading done to them.

While you are talking about what the cards mean, the person having the reading (who from now on I shall call 'the sitter') is the one with all the answers. While you're going through the cards of a reading explaining what each card could potentially mean, the sitter is trying to make sense of what YOU are saying by relating it to their own life. The sitter is the one that will make the connection between the Queen of Diamonds and her aunt Doris once you've explained a 'powerful and influential woman'. You can't make that connection.

The sitter is the one who will listen to you explain 'tough times in the past', but she is also the one who will explain to you exactly why they were tough. The sitter will help you decipher readings that don't seem to make much sense to you at all because you don't know what the sitter is thinking, or understand their dreams, hopes, ambitions and anxieties as well as they do. The sitter is the one who has to make sense of what YOU are saying. She needs to tell you her feelings about the reading as she comes to her own conclusions as you interpret the cards, and she interprets your interpretation!

The sitter is the one who holds the truth and she is the only one who knows which themes, stories and cards are resonating with her. You can interpret the cards as much as you like, but you need the sitter to add the final layer of meaning. Without it, you really do just have stories of imagined futures devoid of relevance to the sitter. The sitter adds the relevance.

Which court card are you?

In a previous revision question I asked a question 'Which court card describes you?' Think about this for a minute. If you had to pick a court card out for yourself, which one would you choose? Which one do you relate to? Which one speaks to you? Which one feels 'right' to you? Which one 'feels' like you?

<u>Action</u>: **Sort out the cards from your working deck into their relative suits. Remove the court cards and choose ONE of these that you feel represents you. Place it down in front of you.**

It's an important question because it challenges you to look at the 'character' of each court card and treat it as an entire person. The court cards are somewhat two dimensional, but it's not that hard to pick the 'closest' to you. I always pick the Jack of Hearts for myself. I'm far too old for the Jack of Hearts, but the King of Hearts just never feels right. It's just one of those things. I think I'll always feel like a kid. You may feel the same way.

Let's take this idea a step further. I hope you've got a good grasp of the card meanings at this stage - this next exercise is useful and will help you understand what's going on in your sitter's mind, as well as your own.

Which spot cards are you?

You read it right - I said CARDS plural.

When we come to give a reading both you and the sitter already have at least one court card you can relate to. Because you've thought about this you'll know which card in the deck is 'you', just as I know that I've always felt that the card that represents me is the Jack of Hearts. The sitter may or may not know which card is 'her'.

Human beings are far more complicated and multi-dimensional than one court card. When someone is having a reading, individual cards speak to them because they push their buttons - they 'shine light' on their existing hopes and fears. Some of them match their hopes and fears exactly.

It's easy to imagine that we are all walking sets of playing cards, the different aspects of our characters reflected in various suits and numbers. It's time to take a moment to think about which cards describe YOU the best.

If you had to pick out a Diamond to describe you, which would it be? *(My choice: 8♦)*

Action: Go through the Diamonds and choose your Diamond aspect. Lay it down.

If you had to pick out a Club to describe you, which would it be? *(My choice: 7♣)*

Action: Go through the Clubs and choose your Clubs aspect. Lay it down.

If you had to pick out a Heart to describe you, which would it be? *(My choice: 5♥)*

Action: Go through the Hearts and choose your Hearts aspect. Lay it down.

If you had to pick out a Spade to describe you, which would it be? *(My choice: 9♠)*

Action: Go through the Spades and choose your Spades aspect. Lay it down.

You need to really sit down and think about this - it's a fascinating exercise and shows that some cards are far closer to your own character than others. As you will discover while going through this process, it's almost impossible not to flatter yourself - yet some of the choices are quite tricky when you are only allowed one of each suit.

To illustrate this concept, here are my reasons for choosing my particular cards:

I chose the Eight of Diamonds as my Diamond aspect. I nearly chose the Three of Diamonds as I like to think I'm good at my best when I'm creating and bringing new things into the world (like this book!). However I decided to go with the Eight of Diamonds as this shows a similar yet more dynamic side to me - I'm a people person, and I have the drive to go out and do things and get things started. I'm not a rich guy, but I do think I have a kind of power although it's hardly financial. But I do have energy and drive.

What's quite interesting about all this is how much I saw myself in all the other Diamonds - most of the cards touch on an aspect of our character to a certain extent, yet it's a case of how much. I could give you reasons why every Diamond was like me if I had to! Yet the Eight of Diamonds seems to sum me up the best.

I chose the Seven of Clubs as my Club aspect. For me this is a no-brainer. My work is creative first and foremost, and this drives everything I do. I can't help it, and like many people like me I do sometimes think there's a link between creating new things and the unknowable. So it's kind of like the connection you make with the universe when you create something. Rather fanciful, but as you will find, it's hard not to speak in grand gestures when you are talking about yourself! After all, there is no greater topic.

So the Clubs was easy for me, I didn't even have to think about it.

I chose the Five of Hearts as my Heart aspect. I nearly chose the Two of Hearts because I'm rather fanciful and prone to romantic notions of world peace and that sort of thing. However, the Seven of Hearts is also strong for me - quite a spiritual card, but for me it's more a kind of 'love heals all evil' type of feeling. But I chose the Five of Hearts and once again this is about being creative - I'm best when I am in stable surroundings, surrounded by people I love and I do my best work this way. In fact the Three of Hearts is quite attractive too, and so is the Six! But I think the Five of Hearts is my best match.

With the Hearts more than any other suit I find myself wanting to pick more than one. You may feel the same - however, you may find that a totally different suit becomes your 'favourite' to chose from.

I chose the Nine of Spades as my Spades aspect. We all have a side to us that we wish was better. We all make mistakes and worry about our shortcomings. Or do we? If you can't see any shortcomings in your own personality then you're probably either very lucky or delusional.

Personally I found the Nine of Spades pretty easy to relate to - it's about finding it hard to finish things and floundering at the last minute. Well, this book has had its fair share of stumbling blocks and I'm amazed I was able to finish it. But also I would say that one of my biggest failings isn't that I never finish anything, but that I find finishing anything so incredibly difficult. So for me as I see it, my Spades aspect has to be the Nine of Spades.

Hopefully my explanation of the cards that I chose for myself has helped you see what I'm talking about - certain cards can't help but represent some aspect of our own character.

Now you've chosen cards to represent your personality, let's turn the attention to your life as it stands right now!

Which spot cards describe your current situation?

What's going on in your life? What's bugging you? What's making you happy? What are your concerns, hopes and fears?

Think for a moment about everything that's going on in your life right now. You're now going to pick a card from each suit that you feel represents your current situation at this moment in time.

Some of the cards you pick for your current situation may be the same cards as you have chosen for your character aspect. If they're not, lay the new card beneath the previous one.

This is a harder exercise than the previous one. We all know what we're like, but choosing a card from each suit to describe our life as it stands is quite a bit harder. If you find it difficult, don't be too rigid about what you think of as 'now'. Think of it like a snapshot of what's happened in your life over the last couple of months, where you think it's all going for the next two months with the present moment sandwiched in between.

If you had to pick out a Diamond to describe your current situation, which would it be?

Action: Go through the Diamonds and choose your current Diamond aspect.
(My choice: A♦ *)*

If you had to pick out a Club to describe your current situation, which would it be?

Action: Go through the Clubs and choose your current Clubs aspect.
(My choice: 3♣ *)*

If you had to pick out a Heart to describe your current situation, which would it be?

Action: Go through the Hearts and choose your current Hearts aspect.
(My choice: 4♥ *)*

If you had to pick out a Spade to describe your current situation, which would it be?

Action: Go through the Spades and choose your current Spades aspect.
(My choice: 5♠ *)*

As before, lay these cards in front of you beneath the others.

It's almost impossible to create this current situation layout without thinking about the future. We always think of the past leading up to the present moment, but in our minds we are always thinking about the future and it's the carrot that moves us along. We are not just a sum of where we've been and where we are - we are also made up of where we're going (or more importantly, where we *think* we're going). So it's natural to find that you want to pick cards that touch on your future hopes and aspirations. When you're doing this exercise however, try and stop that happening and pick cards that as close as possible describe your life right now.

Here are my reasons for choosing my particular 'current situation' cards:

I chose the Ace of Diamonds because I feel like I've come full cycle into a time of fresh starts both financially and creatively. I chose the Three of Clubs because in my creative work there are new ideas and projects which are (finally) going to see the light of day. I chose the Four of Hearts because emotionally I feel like I'm on a very stable footing right now with 'where I'm at' and especially with my family, and I've chosen the Five of Spades as the biggest problem I've had recently (and still have to this particular moment) is one of expanding beyond the confines of my own life as it stands and feel a bit stuck. The other cards reflect the notion that this period is coming to an end.

Which spot cards describe your 'perfect outcome'?

We've chosen a court card to represent us, a card of each suit to describe our character and a card of each suit to describe our current situation. Finally we're going to pick out a card of each suit to describe where we'd like to be in the future. The future we're describing could be a year, two years or ten years away, it's entirely open. But it's important and useful to have some kind of goal or at the very least a direction of some kind.

Of course the Spades don't really have a 'perfect outcome'. When you pick a Spade for this section, chose the one you'd like to have control over.

If you had to pick out a Diamond to describe your perfect outcome, which would it be?

Action: Go through the Diamonds and choose your outcome Diamond aspect.
(My choice: 9♦*)*

If you had to pick out a Club to describe your perfect outcome, which would it be?

Action: Go through the Clubs and choose your outcome Club aspect.
(My choice: 9♣*)*

If you had to pick out a Heart to describe your perfect outcome, which would it be?

Action: Go through the Hearts and choose your outcome Heart aspect.
(My choice: 2♥*)*

If you had to pick out a Spade to describe your perfect outcome, which would it be?

Action: Go through the Spades and choose your outcome Spade aspect.
(My choice: 10♠*)*

This exercise is fairly easy, and most people will pick higher cards like nines and tens. If you're being honest with yourself however, it is possible to pick lower cards that have just as much meaning if not more than the higher cards. We all want to live happily ever after, but if you treat 'the future' during this exercise as a place not too far in the distant future it might help you choose more insightful cards for yourself.

Here are my reasons for choosing my particular 'perfect outcome' cards:

I chose the Nine of Diamonds because I'd like everything in my life right now to get up to speed financially as well as the power to go with it. I chose the Nine of Clubs for the same reasons. I didn't chose the Tens because I still feel that the final goal, whatever that may be, is further along than I can envisage. Right now I'd just like things to kick off into a whirlwind of activity after a long period of stagnation. I chose the Two of Hearts for the same reasons I chose the Jack of Hearts to represent me. And I chose the Ten of Spades because like most people I'd like a clear run with no obstacles of any kind!

Jack of Hearts - My court card
First row - My aspects
Second row - My current situation
Third row - My perfect outcome

My personal layout after having chosen all my cards

By now you'll have given most of the cards in the deck a lot of thought as you try and pick out the cards that are relevant to you and your life. Hopefully it's given you lots of food for thought and forced you to be extremely honest with yourself. Unlike a reading there's nothing random about choosing your own cards and they'll be entirely representative of what you think about yourself, your current situation and where you'd like to be.

So what does this have to do with readings? Well, everything. Now you've given yourself some time to reflect on the cards that resonate with you, you're going to have a much easier time working out how other people connect with the cards and their meanings. Everyone who you give a reading to has their own internal set of cards that reflect their personality, situations and dreams. When you start a reading these cards are hidden, but during a reading they are revealed to both you and the sitter. It is up to you to identify which cards have the most meaning to the sitter, and help them open up to these possibilities.

As you have probably found doing this exercise, being honest with yourself using the cards as a vehicle is actually fairly easy - it may be hard to choose exactly which cards explain who you are and where you're going, but the process itself reveals an honesty that you may not have experienced in yourself for a while. If you've gone through this exercise, you are now looking at a set of cards that explain who you think you are, a set of cards of where you think you are, and a final set of cards that show you where you'd like to be. You may discover that you've neglected to think about where you'd like to be for quite some time!

How often are you this truthful with yourself? Perhaps often, perhaps never. But I think you'd agree it's an extremely interesting, occasionally insightful and a potentially eye-opening exercise. You may have even surprised yourself. The best readings should be like this for our sitter. Although the cards are shuffled and there is a random element to a reading, there is nothing at all random about the way the sitter thinks or feels. They will act and react according to their own internal deck. Everyone who comes for a reading is going to see cards during the process that exactly match their own lives. People have many aspects, and the cards reflect that.

To put it simply, the sitters internal cards are the master cards that influence their thoughts about a reading. Don't be afraid to ask the sitter's opinion - in fact you should welcome and encourage it.

Having gone through this process I hope you can see how useful it has been and how trusting and open people can become (including you!) when you sit with them to decipher a reading. You must respect their openness and not abuse it.

Go through this chapter again once in a while and repeat the whole process. As you and your life changes, so will the cards you choose for yourself. You may want to keep a note of the cards you pick for yourself over time to compare the difference.

CHAPTER 9 - MORE ON READINGS

Although we've been talking about readings through this whole book I thought I should talk a little bit about how to conduct a reading for someone else. It's mostly common sense, but it's here should you be wondering how I do things.

Choosing the cards

If you've got this far in the book you've probably shuffled the cards hundreds of times and picked out many cards at random. There is no hard and fast rule about how you should do this either for yourself or someone else.

When I'm giving a reading for someone else I let them shuffle the cards and then spread the cards face down in front of them, letting them draw three cards out at random, turning them face up as they are chosen before gathering up the remainder of the cards and putting them to one side. The reading can then begin.

Some books say you should always draw the chosen cards out with the left hand but I don't take much notice about stuff like that. As long as the cards are chosen randomly I'm happy.

Sometimes you'll find that in the process of shuffling the cards the sitter will accidentally drop a card or a card will make itself known in some other accidental way. If this happens I place these cards to one side, and although they don't become the focus of the main reading I bear these cards in mind. They can be interesting to talk about once the main reading is over, and they can give additional insights to the main bulk of the reading.

General readings vs question readings

In the last chapter I talked about how everyone brings their own set of internal cards to the reading. When you are giving a general reading you can explore the cards in the reading with no set purpose - you can just see where the cards take you and the sitter and let the conversation develop.

However should the sitter have a specific question in mind this is somewhat different - the question is in effect an invisible 'first' card and the subsequent cards that are laid out are shedding light on this question.

If you know the question that the sitter is thinking of then you can do one of two things. You can simply relate every card in the reading back to the question, or you can pick a card for the question before the cards are shuffled and lay that out first as the main focus. Most questions are pretty simple and choosing a card to represent them is usually pretty straightforward.

Even if you decide not to physically take a card from the deck that represents the sitter's question, it can be useful to at least think about which cards their question could connect to before the reading starts.

Getting Unstuck

There will be times when you're doing a reading where you get 'stuck'. As you've probably noticed in some of the examples over the course of this book, there are moments where there just doesn't seem to be enough information about certain aspects of a reading. This can happen when too many similar cards appear together, more than one court card shows up and for a host of other reasons. What to do?

Just because you're conducting a three card reading doesn't mean you can't use more cards. The simplest method for expanding an unclear section of a reading is to draw another card from the deck, using this new card as an additional influence.

For instance, back in Chapter Seven, example #6 (page 63) and example #10 (page 67) I found it harder than usual to figure out what the reading was trying to tell me. Drawing an extra card during either of these readings would have helped considerably.

I try and be sparing but with particularly troublesome or conflicting readings I'll draw up to a couple more cards, laying each card on top of the cards in question and using these new cards to continue exploring the theme in question. You could draw as many new cards as you want, but whatever spread I'm using I always try and exhaust all avenues of discussion before drawing new cards. Drawing extra cards can make you lazy so I try and only do this as a last resort when I'm really stuck.

Sometimes when you're doing a three card reading it will bring up ideas that the sitter wants to explore further and deeper, for instance you may come across a court card but their intentions are somewhat vague in the current reading. An easy way to continue is to simply use this court card (or whatever card needs to be explored further) as the first card of a new reading. It's quite easy to keep doing overlapping readings like this, exploring avenues and seeing where they lead.

Don't be scared to do what you feel is right at the time. If you want to do a whole new reading, feel free. If you want to extend a three card reading to four or five cards, don't let me stop you! When you're exploring the cards during a reading you should feel in control, and as it's your reading you can do as you see fit.

Creating conversation

Some people talk incessantly during a reading yet others say very little - even nothing. You won't have any problems with the talkers, those readings can be the most fun and when you're giving a reading with someone very open it's very rare that you won't 'get somewhere'.

More often than not you'll be giving readings to people who open up as the reading goes along, so you must encourage them to talk. In the same way that you'll find it hard to get a word in when you're dealing with a 'talker', you must also not let yourself fall into the same trap - you need to encourage the sitter to participate as opposed to being a passive observer, and to enable that to happen you must talk slowly and leave pauses and encourage dialogue.

A simple 'Does that make sense?' or 'I'm not quite sure what this bit here all means...' is all it takes. After all, the sitter wants to make sense of it all and as long as you haven't sold yourself as the 'all seeing oracle' they know that they're going to have to speak up if they're to make the most of the reading. Give them the space to do so.

Of course sometimes you get people who don't say a word no matter how much you encourage them. If that happens your knowledge of the cards will certainly be tested! The best thing to do in these situations is cover as many bases as possible in the hope that you hit a nerve. One thing for certain is that nothing will be lost on someone this shy - they will remember every word.

CHAPTER 10 - BEYOND THE 3 CARD READING

I haven't mentioned other ways of giving readings other than the three card reading as I think it's important to practice getting as much out of as few cards as possible. As you give more readings you'll find that a three card reading can feel somewhat limiting. You always have the choice to draw more cards onto your three cards, but sometimes it's more interesting and useful to use a different spread.

The nine card reading

This is pretty self explanatory and is quite fun to do once you've got the hang of three card readings. Instead of doing a three card reading with three singular cards you lay down *three sets* of *three cards*!

You read each set of three on their own, and can either think of them as past/present/future or treat them as in the three card reading with each set influencing the previous set.

In effect you're doing three three card readings three times. Take a look over all the cards, assess which suits appear the most, which numbers appear the most and the general lay of the red cards versus black cards. After having gone through lots of three card readings, this reading is a natural extension and can be used for general readings as easily as question readings.

Nine card reading

The sevens spread

This is similar to the previous reading method but this time we use seven sets of three cards, with each set being given a particular area of focus.

Set One: State of mind
Set Two: Family
Set Three: Desires
Set Four: Expectations
Set Five: The unexpected
Set Six: Immediate future
Set Seven: Distant future

These can be laid out in an attractive shape across the table and you may or may not decide to pick out the sitters court card before the reading starts, assembling the various sets of cards around their card.

The sevens spread

The star spread

In this spread we lay out and read cards in pairs (and we've certainly had a lot of practice in doing that!) and no pair is considered 'better' than another. The pairs are read in sequence according to their number and the positioning of the cards in the star shape is taken into consideration during the final stages of the reading.

The client's card is the focus as the centre of this spread.

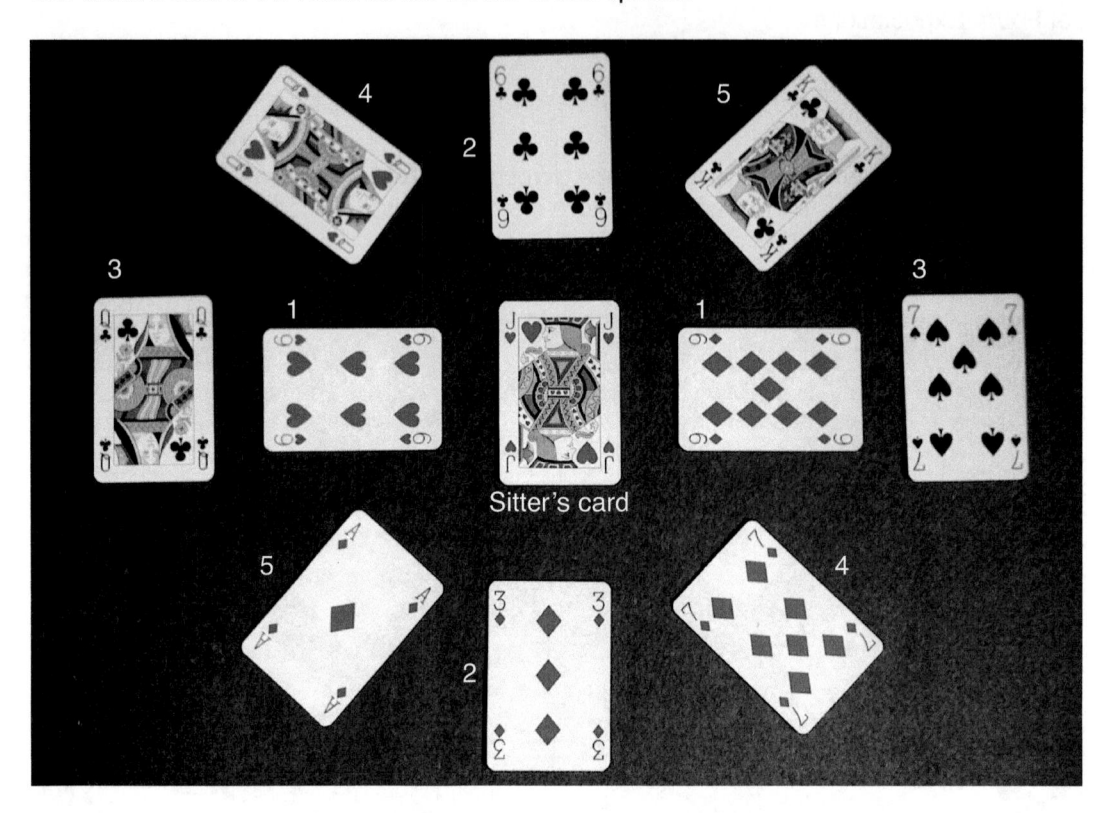

The star spread

This spread can all be extended to thirteen cards by adding a final pair above and below the top and bottom cards (the twos).

Other spreads

There are a huge amount of spreads to choose from and you will have no difficulty finding new ones in other books and across the internet. Experiment with as many as possible to find out which ones you like the best. Even make your own up!

Personally I'm not a huge fan of giant spreads where each pile or section is given its own meaning. I prefer to use spreads where things are more vague and it's up to me and the sitter to decipher what's going on. I have always found forcing a meaning on a set of cards somewhat limiting. Please don't let that stop you from discovering and developing your own spreads and using others that you may come across.

CHAPTER 11 - NUMEROLOGY AND OTHER SYSTEMS

You could write a whole book on the numbers one to nine, and of course there are many books on numerology on the market. During this book I've kept things simple so that the focus has been more about cartomancy and less about numerology, even though the two are inextricably linked. However you may well have come to this book knowing something about numerology, and you may well be familiar with other systems such as horoscopes.

Any other knowledge you have about other systems can and should be applied to your knowledge of cartomancy and its card numbers to enrich the experience for you and your sitter.

The best way to gain a deeper understanding of cartomancy is to gain a deeper knowledge of numerology. It is out of the scope of this book to delve into the thousands of associations and connections that the numbers have with other systems, but there now follows an short easy reference guide to help those of you whose first contact with numerology has been this book.

Apart from the numbers one to nine, there are two master numbers - eleven and twenty two. These are considered highly auspicious when they appear anywhere. Of course the only time they can appear in a reading is when you start adding card values together, but it's something you should be aware of.

Numbers / Planets / Star signs

ONE - Sun / Leo

KEYWORDS: Independence, loneliness, creativity, originality, dominance, leadership, impatience

Character traits: Powerful personality. Individualistic, intensely original and creative. An inspiring leader and a pioneer. Efficient, determined and good at initiating new projects.

TWO - Moon / Cancer

KEYWORDS: Quiet, passive, diplomatic, co-operation, comforting, soothing, intuitive, compromising, patient

Character traits: Good-natured, sympathetic, understanding and helpful - a good shoulder to cry on. Gregarious yet shy and timid. Likes detail, routine and stability and may be worried by sudden changes.

THREE - Mercury / Gemini

KEYWORDS: Charming, out-going, self-expressive, extroverted, abundance, active, energetic, proud

Character traits: Centre of attention, show off, loves to be admired yet fairly sensitive. Over-stretches himself. Pleasure seeking, may be wasteful with money.

FOUR - Venus & Earth / Taurus

KEYWORDS: Harmony, truth, justice, order, discipline, practicality, material world, dedication

Character traits: Steady and reliable. Practical and sensible, calm. Good at managing and saving money. Courageous and honest and ethical in all that they do. Responsible reliable and extremely dependable.

FIVE - Mars / Aries

KEYWORDS: New directions, excitement, change adventure

Character traits: Versatile, resourceful, clever and amusing. Good company, good with words, optimistic. Lively, inquiring and outgoing. Makes friends and money easily. Lives for the moment. Loves adventure and travel, change and anything new. A free spirit, impatient with rules, laws and conventions.

SIX - Venus & Asteroid belt / Pisces

KEYWORDS: Love, harmony, perfection, marriage / family, tolerance, public service

Character traits: Equilibrium,. enjoys peace between people. Values comfort and ease and enjoys beautiful things. Negotiator. Peace-maker.

SEVEN - Jupiter / Aquarius

KEYWORDS: Spirituality, completeness, solitary, isolation, introspection

Character traits: Mystic, philosopher. Introspective and thoughtful - sometimes appears aloof. Quiet, intuitive and meditative. Takes the broad view.

EIGHT - Saturn / Capricorn

KEYWORDS: Organisation, business, commerce, immortality, resurrection, new beginnings, success / failure

Character traits: Ambitious for power, status, money, success. May lead to great success or sudden failure. Busy with world affairs. May neglect private life in the search for their material dreams.

NINE - Uranus / Sagittarius

KEYWORDS: Romantic, rebellious, determined, passionate, compassionate, affectionate

Character traits: A humanitarian, fighter for social causes capable of inspired action and of inspiring others. Many interest and sympathies, generous and compassionate. Romantic, high minded and idealistic - a hopeless romantic and lover of beauty in all things. Impressionable, intuitive yet independent.

TEN - Pluto / Scorpio

KEYWORDS: See **ONE**

*Character traits: See **ONE** (this is the character come full circle)*

ELEVEN - Neptune / Libra

KEYWORDS: See **TWO**

*Character traits: As **TWO** but more spiritual.*

TWELVE - 12th planet / Virgo

KEYWORDS: See **THREE**

*Character traits: As **THREE** but more spiritual.*

TWENTY TWO - Venus & Earth / Taurus

KEYWORDS: See **FOUR**

*Character traits: As **FOUR** but more spiritual.*

CHAPTER 12 - CARTOMANCY AS LANGUAGE

In chapter eight we discussed how picking out cards that represent your own personality, situation and hopes for the future could give you a greater insight into the cards. We've also talked about how it's useful to think of everyone as having their own 'internal deck' that they bring to the table when they come for a reading.

As a final thought for this book I wanted to touch on the idea of the cards as a language. We interpret the cards to create stories, which when discussed with the sitter can help us discover the themes and ideas that are the most pertinent in their lives. In this respect the cards are like hieroglyphics - each one representing a concept or theme that when strung together can create a narrative. As the one giving the reading, you supply some of the 'glue' that can piece these ideas together, along with the help of the sitter who adds context and truth.

Thinking of the cards in this way is interesting as we are able to see them as the building blocks for story telling and extemporisation. They are a language unto themselves.

With that in mind I want to leave you with the idea that you can actually reverse engineer this concept by starting with a story first, and then try to piece together the cards that tell the story.

For instance, if I told you this little story -

' A relationship is being put under intense pressure due to money related worries although they will be resolved'

- then you could describe that story, using the suits of the cards only as

Hearts **Spades** *Diamonds*

This is simply one of the early suit readings from page 22, but in reverse - we're thinking of the story first and trying to work out how we'd explain that using the language of the cards.

On page 67 I described a fun exercise, to go through the pack creating a continuous narrative from the cards and seeing how far you could go before you ran out of ideas. This is a bit like that, but I'm talking now about describing *existing* stories. We've done it with ourselves to a certain extent when we had to choose some cards to represent our current situation in chapter eight. Now I want you to start applying it to your friends, people you know, stories you hear and things you read in the paper, on the internet and see on the news.

Start using the cards to describe every day events.

For instance, if I told you this story -

'A fair woman with a heart of gold hears some good news from a lady at work'

- then you could sum this story up with these three cards

Queen of Hearts / Six of Hearts / **Queen of Clubs**

or how about this one -

'Some projects at work are taking good shape from stable progress thanks to a young guy whose family connections are a major contributing factor to the success of the project'

- you could use these cards to describe this scenario

Five of Clubs / Jack of Clubs / *Ten of Hearts*

The point of all this is that by starting with the scenario first, it forces you to use the cards as a descriptive story telling language. By thinking about all kinds of things that go on in your life and in the world around you and considering how you might describe those things using the cards, you will gain great insight into how the cards work together, and will start noticing patterns and obvious connections that the cards make when they describe both the big and small events in our lives.

Next time you're watching a news story or reading an article, think for a while about which cards could sum it up. You can practice this no matter where you are or what you're doing. The cards are there to describe the world and the more you play with them them, the more the world of cartomancy will make sense.

CHAPTER 13 - CONCLUSION

Cartomancy is a great thing to learn as it is an interesting gateway into learning about numerology and other card systems such as the Tarot, even though cartomancy itself is a fascinating subject in its own right. Everyone has a pack of cards lying around somewhere, and with the knowledge contained in this book you'll always be good to go when it comes to giving a reading.

Most people know a tiny bit about giving readings with cards, yet most people never get very further than the 'hearts are love' stage. It's a great thing to be able to do, and you get a good feeling when you start really getting to know some of the cards. Instead of just being suits and numbers you'll find entire scenarios, pictures and ideas coming in to your head as soon as you see a card, and if you follow what's in this book you'll soon find it hard to look at any two cards without wanting to put them together to work out what they mean!

I really hope you can use this book as a springboard into learning more about cartomancy and I'm sure you'll have a lot of fun sitting with your friends, family and even clients as you uncover the fascinating secrets that wait for you in every deck of cards.

Good luck!

Julian Moore
April 2011

*For more books on palmistry, graphology,
readings and mentalism please visit*

The Cold Reading Company
http://thecoldreadingcompany.co.uk

Printed in France by Amazon
Brétigny-sur-Orge, FR